Best Garden Plants *for* Missouri

Anita Joggerst • *Don Williamson*

LONE
PINE

Lone Pine Publishing International

The Distributor: Lone Pine Publishing
1808 B Street NW, Suite 140
Auburn, WA, USA 98001
Website: www.lonepinepublishing.com

Library and Archives Canada Cataloguing in Publication

Joggerst, Anita, 1948–
  Best garden plants for Missouri / Anita Joggerst, Don Williamson.

Includes index.
ISBN-13: 978–976–8200–12–9

  1. Plants, Ornamental—Missouri. 2. Gardening—Missouri.
I. Williamson, Don, 1962– II. Title.

SB453.2.M8J63 2006   635.909778   C2006–903584–9

Scanning & Digital Film: Elite Lithographers Co.

Photography: All photos by Tamara Eder, Tim Matheson, Laura Peters and Allison Penko, with the following exceptions:
Doris Baucom 31a; Pam Beck 140a; David Cavagnaro 21a, 140b, 167a&b; Joan de Grey 133a; Therese D'Monte 136b; Don Doucette 107b; Derek Fell 64a, 73a, 76a&b, 101a, 109a, 118a, 127, 135a, 136a, 138a, 162b, 164b; Erika Flatt 9b, 90a, 130b, 134a, 166b; Anne Gordon 21b, 61b, 137b; Bailey Nursery Roses 110a; Conard-Pyle Roses 110b, 118b; Saxon Holt 64b, 137a; Jackson & Perkins 111a; Duncan Kelbaugh 130a; Liz Klose 160a; Debra Knapke 125a; Dawn Loewen 69a; Janet Loughrey 109b, 122b, 135b, 138b; Marilynn McAra 133b; Steve Nikkila 99a; Kim O'Leary 13b, 24a, 44a&b, 74a, 91b, 129a; Photos.com 139a; PPA 62a; Robert Ritchie 42b, 51b, 82a&b, 84a, 94b, 96a, 103b, 114a, 123a; Leila Sidi 139b; Joy Spurr 119a; Peter Thompstone 22a, 30b; Mark Turner 0201199, 101b; Mark Turner PR 0104043, 162a; Don Williamson 131a&b, 142a; Tim Wood 71a, 80a, 104a, 107a.

This book is not intended as a 'how-to' guide for eating garden plants. No plant or plant extract should be consumed unless you are certain of its identity and toxicity and of your potential for allergic reactions.

PC: P13

Table of Contents

Introduction. 4

Annuals 11

Perennials 40

Trees & Shrubs. 69

Roses 109

Vines 119

Bulbs 129

Herbs. 141

Ferns, Grasses & Groundcovers 151

Glossary 171
Index 172
About the Authors & Acknowledgments 176

Introduction

Starting a garden can seem like a daunting task. Which plants should you choose? Where should you put them in the garden? This book is intended to give beginning gardeners the information they need to have success in planning and planting gardens. It describes a wide variety of plants and provides basic information such as where and how to plant.

Missouri exhibits a wide diversity of ecological regions, from the Northern Plains through the Ozark Plateau and down into the Mississippi Alluvial Plain in the Bootheel. Each of these broad areas presents its own unique challenges. One of the biggest challenges is selecting plants that can handle our climate, especially our cold winters in the Northern Plains region. USDA hardiness zones are based on how cold it gets in winter. Plants are rated based on the zones in which they grow successfully, but cold is not the only factor influencing winter survival. A winter temperature of -5° F is very different with snow cover than without, in soggy soil or in dry soil and following a hot summer or a long, cold, wet one. These factors have more influence on the survival of plants than does temperature.

Spring and fall frost dates are often used when discussing climate and gardening. They let us know generally when, statistically, to expect the last frost in spring and the first frost in fall. The last frost date in spring combined with the first frost date in fall allows us to predict the length of the growing season. Your local garden center should be able to provide you with local hardiness zones and frost date information. Refer to the map on p. 5 for general hardiness zone information.

Getting Started

When planning your garden, start with a quick analysis of the garden as it is now. Plants have different requirements, and it is best to put the right plant in the right place rather than to change your garden to suit the plants you want.

Knowing which parts of your garden receive the most and least amounts of sunlight will help you choose the proper plants and decide where to put them.

The amount of sunlight a site receives is generally described with the following terms: full sun (direct, unobstructed light for all or most of the day), partial shade (direct sun for about half the day and shade for the rest), light shade (shade for all or most of the day, with some sun filtering through to ground level) and full shade (no direct sunlight). Most plants prefer a specific amount of light, but many can adapt to a range of light levels.

Plants use the soil to hold themselves upright, but they also rely on the many resources it holds: air, water, nutrients, organic matter and a host of microbes. The particle size of the soil influences the amount of air, water and nutrients it can hold. Sand, with the largest particles, has a lot of air space and allows water and nutrients to drain quickly. Clay, with the smallest particles, is high in nutrients but has very little air space. Water is therefore slow to penetrate clay and slow to drain from it.

Soil acidity or alkalinity (measured on the pH scale) influences the nutrients available to plants. A pH of 7 is neutral; a lower pH is more acidic. Most plants prefer a soil with a pH of 5.5–7.5. Soil testing kits are available at most garden centers, and soil samples can be sent to testing facilities for a more thorough analysis.

Compost is one of the best and most important amendments you can add to any type of soil. Compost improves soil by adding organic matter and nutrients, introducing soil microbes, increasing water retention and improving drainage. Compost can be purchased, or you can make it in your own backyard.

Microclimates are small areas that are generally warmer or colder than the surrounding area. Buildings, fences, trees and other large structures can provide extra shelter in winter and may trap heat in summer, thus creating a warmer microclimate. The bottoms of hills are usually colder than the tops, but they may not be as windy. Take advantage of these areas when you plan your garden and choose your plants; in a warm, sheltered location, you may even be able to successfully grow out-of-zone plants.

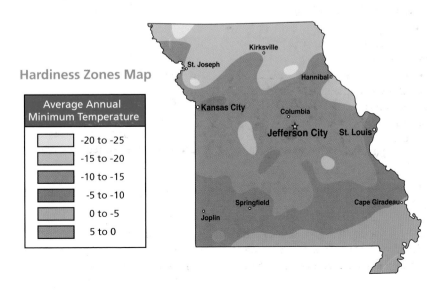

Hardiness Zones Map

Average Annual Minimum Temperature

- -20 to -25
- -15 to -20
- -10 to -15
- -5 to -10
- 0 to -5
- 5 to 0

Kirksville
St. Joseph
Hannibal
Kansas City
Columbia
Jefferson City
St. Louis
Springfield
Cape Giradeau
Joplin

Selecting Plants

It's important to purchase healthy plants that are free of pests and diseases. Such plants will establish quickly in your garden and won't introduce problems that may spread to other plants. You should have a good idea of what the plant is supposed to look like—the color and shape of the leaves and the habit of the plant—and then inspect the plant for signs of disease or infestation.

The majority of plants available for sale are container grown. It is an efficient way for nurseries and greenhouses to grow plants, but plants grown in a restricted space for too long can become pot bound, with their roots densely encircling the inside of the pot. Avoid purchasing pot-bound plants, because they are often stressed and can take longer to establish. In some cases, they may not establish at all. It is often possible to remove pots temporarily to look at the condition of the roots. You can check for soil-borne insects and rotten roots at the same time.

Planting Basics

The following tips apply to all plants:

- Prepare the garden before planting. Dig over the soil, pull up any weeds and make any needed amendments before you begin planting, if possible. These preparations may be more difficult in established beds to which you want to add a single plant. The prepared area should be at least twice the size of the rootball of the plant you want to put in and preferably larger.

- Know the mature size. Place your plants based on how big they will grow rather than how big they are when you plant them. Large plants should have enough room to mature without interfering with walls, roof overhangs, power lines, walkways or other plants.

- Accommodate the rootball. If you prepared your planting spot ahead of time, your planting hole will only need to be big enough to accommodate the root ball with the roots spread out slightly.

- Unwrap the roots. It is best to remove any container before planting to give the roots a chance to spread out naturally when planted. In particular, you should remove plastic containers, fiber pots, wire and burlap before planting trees. Fiber pots decompose very slowly, if at all, and wick moisture away from the plant. Synthetic burlap won't decompose, and wire can strangle the roots as they mature. The only exceptions to this rule are peat pots and pellets used to start annuals and vegetables; they decompose and can be planted with the young transplants.

- Plant at the same depth in the soil. Plants generally like to grow at a certain level in relation to the soil and should

Gently remove container.

Ensure proper planting depth.

Backfill with soil.

be planted at the same level they were growing at before you transplanted them.

- Settle the soil with water. Good contact between the roots and the soil is important, but if you press the soil down too firmly, as often happens when you step on the soil, you can cause compaction, which reduces the movement of water through the soil and leaves very few air spaces. Instead, pour water in as you fill the hole with soil. The water will settle the soil evenly without allowing it to compact.

- Identify your plants. Keep track of what's what in your garden by putting a tag next to each plant when you plant it or by making a sketch map with plant names and locations. Otherwise, it is very easy to forget exactly what you planted and where you planted it.

- For newly transplanted plants, water every other day for at least three weeks. After that period, the roots of the plant should have entered the prepared soil, and water twice a week for a month is sufficient unless you see the plant wilt. You should then be able to go to once a week or longer between watering, depending on the plant's requirements.

- For established plants, water deeply and infrequently. It's better to water deeply once every week or two rather than to water lightly more often. Deep watering forces roots to grow as they search for water and helps them survive dry spells when water bans may restrict your watering regime. Always check the root zone before you water. More gardeners overwater than underwater.

Annuals

Annuals are planted anew each year and are expected to last only for a single growing season. Their flowers and decorative foliage provide bright splashes of color and can fill in spaces around immature trees, shrubs and perennials.

Many annuals are grown from seed and can be started directly in the garden or bought as bedding plants in small packs of four or six. They are easy to plant. The roots quickly fill the space in these small packs, so the small rootball should be broken up before planting. For most annuals, split the ball in two up the center or run your thumb up each side to break up the roots. Some annuals dislike having their roots disturbed; these plants are often direct-sown or grown in peat pots or pellets to minimize root disturbance.

Perennials

Perennials grow for three or more years. They usually die back to the ground each fall and send up new shoots in spring, although some are evergreen. They often have a shorter period of bloom than annuals but require less care.

Settle backfilled soil with water.

Water the plant well.

Add a layer of mulch.

Many perennials benefit from being divided every few years; it keeps them growing and blooming vigorously and can be used to control their spread. Dividing involves digging the plant up, removing dead bits, breaking the plant into several pieces and replanting some or all of the pieces. Extra pieces can be given as gifts to family, friends and neighbors.

Trees & Shrubs

Trees and shrubs provide the bones of the garden. They are often the slowest growing plants, but they usually live the longest. Characterized by leaf type, they may be deciduous or evergreen, and needled or broad-leaved.

Trees should have as little disturbed soil as possible at the bottom of the planting hole. Loose soil settles over time, and sinking even an inch can kill some trees.

Staking, sometimes recommended for newly planted trees, is necessary only for trees over 5' tall.

Pruning is more often required for shrubs than trees. It helps them maintain an attractive shape and can improve blooming. It is a good idea to take a pruning course or to hire or consult with an ISA (International Society of Arboriculture) certified arborist if you have never pruned before.

Trees and shrubs are the backbone of the mixed border.

Roses

Roses are beautiful shrubs with lovely, often-fragrant blooms. Traditionally, most roses only bloomed once in the growing season, but new varieties bloom all, or almost all, summer.

Generally, roses prefer a fertile, well-prepared planting area. A guideline is to prepare a circular area 24" in diameter and 24" deep. Although many roses are quite durable and adapt to poorer conditions, it is best to add plenty of compost or other fertile organic matter. Keep roses well watered during the growing season. Roses, like all shrubs, have specific pruning requirements.

Vines

Vines or climbing plants are useful for screening and shade, especially in a location too small for a tree. They may be woody or herbaceous and annual or perennial.

Most vines need sturdy supports to grow up on. Trellises, arbors, porch railings, fences, walls, poles and trees are all possible supports. If a support is needed, ensure it's in place before you plant to avoid disturbing the roots later.

Bulbs

These plants have fleshy underground storage organs that allow them to survive extended periods of dormancy. They are often grown for the bright splashes of color their flowers provide. They may flower in spring, summer or fall.

Hardy bulbs can be left in the ground and will flower every year, but many popular tender plants also grow from bulbs, corms or tubers. These tender plants are generally lifted from the garden in fall as the foliage dies back, stored in a cool, frost-free location for winter and replanted in spring.

Training vines to climb arbors adds structure to the garden.

Herbs

Herbs may be medicinal or culinary and often both. A few common culinary herbs are listed in this book. Even if you don't cook with them, the often-fragrant foliage adds its aroma to the garden, and the plants have decorative forms, leaves and flowers.

Many herbs have pollen-producing flowers that attract butterflies, bees and hummingbirds to the garden. They also attract predatory insects. These useful insects help to manage your pest problems by feasting on problem insects such as aphids, mealybugs and whiteflies.

Ferns, Grasses & Groundcovers

Many plants are grown for their decorative foliage rather than their flowers. Ornamental grasses, ferns, groundcovers and other foliage plants add a variety of colors, textures and forms to the garden. Many of these are included in other sections of this book, but we have set aside a few for the unique touch their foliage, form and habits add to the garden.

Ferns are ancient plants that have adapted to many different environments. The fern family is a very large group of plants with interesting foliage in a wide array of types and colors. Ferns do not produce flowers; instead, they reproduce by spores borne in interesting structures on the undersides and margins of the leaves. Ferns are generally planted in moist, shaded gardens, but some thrive in dry soil in the deep shade of some trees, such as oak and magnolia.

Ornamental grasses are becoming very popular additions to gardens. Grasses offer a variety of textures and foliage colors for at least three seasons of interest. There is an ornamental grass for every garden situation and condition. Some grasses thrive in any garden condition, from hot and dry to cool and wet, and in all types of soils.

Ornamental grasses have very few insect or disease problems. They require very little maintenance other than cutting the perennial grasses back in fall or spring. If you plan to leave dried grass standing for winter interest, be aware that it can present a fire hazard. Dry grass is highly flammable and should be cut back in fall if it is near a house or other structure.

Groundcovers are often spreading plants with dense growth above and below ground that are used to control soil erosion, to keep weeds at bay and to fill garden areas that are difficult to maintain. Groundcovers can be herbaceous or woody and annual or perennial.

Many herbs grow well in pots.

Ornamental grasses add color, variety and texture.

Pretty well any plant that covers the ground can be used as a groundcover. Vines and plants that are aggressive spreaders make excellent groundcovers, but any plants with dense growth, if enough of them are planted, will serve the purpose. To ensure the ground is completely covered, you may need to space the plants closer together than usual when planting.

Final Comments

We encourage you to visit the outstanding garden shows, botanical gardens, public gardens, arboretums and private gardens (get permission first) we have here in Missouri to see which plants grow best and which ones most catch your interest. A walk through your neighborhood is also a grand way to see which plants might do well in your own garden. Don't be afraid to ask questions.

Missouri has some excellent garden resources. Every county in the state has an office of the University of Missouri Extension. The resources available through these offices are vast and respected. Check out the online site at http://extension.missouri.edu or look in the white pages of the phone book under "University of Missouri" for your county's office.

If you would like to grow something different than your neighbors, there are two programs of which you should be aware. The first is the **Plant of Merit** program, which is an outreach educational program that began at the Missouri Botanical Garden in 1999; it now includes Powell Gardens, the University of Missouri, local garden retailers and wholesalers and members of the landscape industry. The program covers all of Missouri and parts of the surrounding states, promotes reliable but underused plants and encourages ecologically responsible plant diversity. The selected plants do not compete with native plants and do not become invasive. New plants are added every year. The success of the program can be measured by the number of **Emeritus Plants of Merit**—plants previously designated as plants of merit but which are no longer underused, although they are still great choices. More information can be found online at www.plantsofmerit.org. The Missouri Botanical Garden's Kemper Center for Home Gardening is an excellent resource for Missouri gardeners. After checking out the plants of merit at the above link, peruse the wealth of information available online and at the Center.

Grow Native!™ is another good Missouri program that is cosponsored by the Missouri Department of Conservation and the Missouri Department of Agriculture. The program is designed to familiarize people with Missouri native plants and their conservation, and it encourages and promotes their use. Information about Grow Native can be found at www.grownative.org.

Also, don't be afraid to experiment. No matter how many books you read, trying things yourself is the best way to learn and to find out what will grow in your garden. Use the information provided as guidelines—and have fun!

Angelonia
Angelonia

A. angustifolia (above & below)

*A*ngelonia is a heat-loving plant that produces a lot of flowers in many shades of blue, purple and white. The flowers resemble tiny angels.

Growing
Angelonia prefers **full sun** but tolerates a bit of shade. The soil should be **fertile, moist** and **well drained**. Although this plant grows naturally in damp areas, such as along ditches and near ponds, it tolerates drought and heat fairly well. Plant out after the risk of frost has passed.

Tips
Angelonia makes a good addition to an annual or mixed border, where it is most attractive when planted in groups. It is also suitable for pondside or streamside planting.

Also called: angel wings, summer snapdragon
Features: attractive purple, blue, white or bicolored flowers
Height: 12–24" **Spread:** 12"

Recommended
A. angustifolia is a bushy, upright plant with loose spikes of flowers in varied shades of purple. Cultivars with white or bicolored flowers are available. **Angelface Series** (from Proven Winners) plants bear larger flowers and are more compact than the species, reaching 12–18" in height. **Angelmist Series** (from Simply Beautiful) plants are strong growers that reach 18–24" in height and offer fine cut flowers.

The individual flowers look a bit like orchid blossoms, but angelonia is actually in the same family as snapdragon.

Bacopa

Sutera

S. cordata (above & below)

Bacopa is a perennial that is grown as an annual outdoors. It will thrive as a houseplant in a bright room.

Bacopa can make an ordinary hanging basket spectacular. The plethora of tiny, white to pale lavender flowers spill over the sides of the basket, complementing just about any other plant it is growing with.

Growing

Bacopa grows well in **partial shade,** with protection from the hot afternoon sun. The soil should be of **average fertility, humus rich, moist** and **well drained**. Don't allow this plant to dry out, or the leaves will quickly die. Cutting back dead growth may encourage new shoots to form.

Tips

Bacopa is a popular plant for hanging baskets, mixed containers and window boxes. Because it fizzles quickly when the weather gets hot, particularly if you forget to water, it is not recommended as a bedding plant. Plant it where you will see it every day so you will remember to water it.

Recommended

S. cordata is a compact, trailing plant that bears small, white flowers all summer. Cultivars with larger white flowers, lavender flowers or gold and green variegated foliage are available.

Features: decorative white or lavender flowers; foliage; habit
Height: 3–6" **Spread:** 12–20"

Begonia
Begonia

Whether you want beautiful flowers, a compact habit or decorative foliage, there is a begonia to fulfill your shade-gardening needs.

Growing
Begonias grow best in **light shade** or **partial shade**; some wax begonias tolerate sun if the soil is kept moist. Begonias prefer a **fertile, well-drained, neutral to acidic** soil that is **rich in organic matter**. Allow the soil to dry out slightly between waterings, particularly for tuberous begonias. Don't plant begonias before the soil warms in spring, because they may fail to thrive in cold soil.

Tips
All begonias are useful for shaded garden beds and planters. Trailing varieties look great when their flowers are allowed to cascade down. Wax begonias are attractive as edging plants. Rex begonias, with their dramatic foliage, and the DRAGON WING Series are useful as specimen plants.

Recommended
B. x *hybrida* DRAGON WING **Series** plants are heat tolerant and bear deep scarlet to deep pink flowers and angel-winged foliage. DRAGON WING RED ('Bepared') is a Missouri Botanical Garden **Plant of Merit**.

B. **Rex Cultorum Hybrids** (rex begonias) are grown for their dramatic, colorful foliage.

B. x *semperflorens-cultorum* (wax begonias) have pink, white, red or bicolored flowers and green, bronze, reddish or white-variegated foliage.

B. Rex Cultorum hybrids 'Escargot' (above)
B. x *semperflorens-cultorum* (below)

Features: pink, white or red flowers; decorative foliage; easy to grow; low maintenance **Height:** 6–24" **Spread:** 6–24"

Black-Eyed Susan
Rudbeckia

R. hirta 'Becky Mixed' (above), R. hirta (below)

This extremely popular native biennial is a common sight in woodlands, waste areas, prairies, meadows and other wild areas of Missouri.

Black-eyed Susan brightens up any spot in the garden, and its tolerance for heavy soils makes it useful in new developments, where the topsoil is often very thin.

Growing
Black-eyed Susan grows equally well in **full sun** or **partial shade**. The soil should be of **average fertility, humus rich, moist** and **well drained**. This plant tolerates heavy clay soil and hot weather. When grown in loose, moist soil, black-eyed Susan may reseed itself. Plants can be purchased, started from seed early indoors or directly sown around the last spring frost date. Deadhead to prolong blooming.

Tips
Plant black-eyed Susan individually or in groups. Use it in beds and borders, large containers, meadow plantings and wildflower gardens. This plant blooms well, even in the hottest part of the garden. Black-eyed Susan makes a long-lasting vase flower.

Recommended
R. hirta forms a bristly mound of foliage and bears daisy-like, bright yellow flowers with brown centers in summer and fall. A wide variety of cultivars are available, including dwarf plants and double-flowered plants. **'Indian Summer'** has large, single to semi-double, golden yellow flowers on sturdy plants 36" tall and 12–18" wide. The individual flowers of this **Plant of Merit** selection are 6–9" across.

Also called: coneflower, gloriosa daisy
Features: yellow, orange, red, brown or sometimes bicolored flowers with brown or green centers **Height:** 8–36" or more
Spread: 12–20"

Butter Daisy
Melampodium

This tough-as-nails annual is low maintenance, has a very high tolerance to heat, dryness and humidity, and blesses us with bright color from late spring to fall frost.

Growing

Butter daisy grows well in **full sun,** in **well-drained** soil of **average fertility** that has been **amended with compost.** It tolerates partial shade. Keep the soil moist until the plants are established, but let it dry out between waterings. Butter daisy can handle drought, but it does best with some moisture. Sow seed indoors early or sow directly into warm soil in the garden.

Tips

Plant en masse for maximum impact. Dwarf varieties are excellent in containers and for edging beds and borders. Butter daisy mixes well with many annuals and perennials, and it can be dotted throughout the garden for colorful accents.

Recommended

***M. divaricatum** (M. paludosum)* is a bushy, mounding annual with pale green to gray-green leaves that grows 15–24" tall and 12–15" wide. It produces a plethora of star-shaped, bright yellow flowers all season long. Compact cultivars are available, including the **Plant of Merit** selection **'Derby,'** which grows 12–18" tall, 24–36" wide and bears abundant blooms.

M. divaricatum (above & below)

This annual is self-cleaning. It sheds its spent flowers on a regular basis and doesn't require pinching to encourage branching.

Also called: medallion flower
Features: bright yellow flowers; habit; drought tolerance **Height:** 12–24" **Spread:** 12–36"

Calendula

Calendula

C. officinalis 'Apricot Surprise' (above), *C. officinalis* (below)

Calendula is bright and charming, producing attractive flowers in warm colors from summer to fall.

Growing

Calendula does equally well in **full sun** or **partial shade,** in **well-drained** soil of **average fertility**. It prefers cool weather and can withstand a light frost. Young plants are readily available in nurseries. Calendula is easy to start from seed, which is how many gardeners grow it. A second sowing in mid-summer gives a good fall display. Deadhead to prolong blooming and to keep the plants looking neat.

Calendula flowers are popular kitchen herbs that can be added to stews for color or to salads for flavoring.

Tips

This informal plant looks attractive in annual and mixed borders and containers, and it fits easily into the vegetable patch. Calendula offers excellent cut flowers and works well in cottage gardens and large informal beds. Calendula looks great planted in groups of five or more.

Recommended

C. officinalis is a vigorous, tough, upright plant that bears daisy-like, single or double flowers in a wide range of yellow and orange shades. It is a cold-hardy annual and often continues flowering until the ground freezes completely. Several cultivars are available.

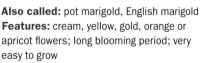

Also called: pot marigold, English marigold
Features: cream, yellow, gold, orange or apricot flowers; long blooming period; very easy to grow
Height: 10–24" **Spread:** 8–20"

Cleome

Cleome

Create a bold and exotic display in your garden with these lovely and unusual flowers.

Growing

Cleomes prefer **full sun** but tolerate partial shade. Any kind of soil is fine, but mix in **plenty of organic matter** to help the soil retain moisture. The plants tolerate drought but perform better if watered regularly. Overwatering causes leggy plants.

Pinch out the tip of the center stem on young plants to encourage branching and more blooms. Deadhead to prolong blooming and reduce prolific self-seeding.

Tips

Cleomes can be planted in groups at the back of a border or in the center of an island bed. They also make an attractive addition to mixed containers.

Recommended

C. hassleriana is a tall, upright plant with strong, supple, thorny stems. The foliage and flowers have a strong scent. **'Sparkler Blush'** is a dwarf cultivar with pink flowers that fade to white.

C. serrulata (Rocky Mountain bee plant) **'Solo'** is thornless, grows 12–18" tall and bears large pink and white blooms.

C. hassleriana (above & below)

Cleomes keep blooming after many other plants have finished, providing hummingbirds with nectar well into fall.

Also called: spider flower
Features: attractive, scented foliage; purple, pink or white flowers; thorny stems
Height: 10"–5' **Spread:** 12–36"

Coleus

Solenostemon

S. scutellarioides mixed cultivars (above & below)

Take cuttings from a coleus mother plant—they root easily in a glass of water—and overwinter them inside.

There is a coleus for everyone. This plant has almost limitless colors, textures and variations.

Growing

Coleus prefers **light shade** or **partial shade,** but it tolerates full shade if it isn't too dense and full sun if the plants are watered regularly. The soil should be **average to fertile, humus rich, moist** and **well drained**.

Place the seeds in a refrigerator for one or two days before planting them on the soil surface; the cold helps break seed dormancy, and they need light to germinate. The seedlings will be green at first, with variegation developing as the plants mature.

Tips

Coleus looks dramatic when grouped in beds, borders and mixed containers or when planted as edging.

Pinch off the flower buds when they develop, because coleus tends to stretch out and become less attractive after it blooms.

Recommended

S. scutellarioides forms a bushy mound of slightly toothed to very ruffled, multi-colored foliage. Dozens of cultivars are available, but many cannot be started from seed. New varieties are available that better tolerate full sun and have larger, more colorful foliage.

Features: brightly colored foliage
Height: 6–36" or more
Spread: usually equal to height

Cosmos

Cosmos

Cosmos are low-cost, low-maintenance cottage garden flowers that are easy to grow and never fail to delight. They can handle the toughest, driest conditions we have in Missouri.

Growing

Cosmos like **full sun** and **well-drained** soil with **poor to average fertility**. Plant out after the last frost. Overfertilizing and overwatering can reduce the number of flowers. Remove spent flowers to encourage more blooming. These plants often self-seed.

Tips

Carefree, colorful, lacy and drought tolerant, cosmos make attractive additions to cottage gardens, beds and borders. They look great when mass planted in informal settings.

Push twiggy branches into the ground when the plants are young and allow the stems to grow up between them; the mature plant will hide the branches. To avoid the need for staking, plant cosmos against a fence or in a sheltered location—or grow short varieties.

Recommended

C. bipinnatus (annual cosmos) is an erect plant with fine, fern-like foliage. It and its many cultivars bear magenta, rose, pink, white or bicolored flowers, usually with yellow centers.

C. sulphureus (yellow cosmos) is a small, dense plant that bears gold, orange, scarlet or yellow flowers. Sow directly in the garden. Cultivars are available.

C. bipinnatus (above), *C. sulphureus* (below)

Cosmos blooms make lovely, long-lasting additions to cut flower arrangements.

Features: magenta, rose, pink, white, gold, yellow, orange, scarlet or bicolored flowers; fern-like foliage; easy to grow; low maintenance
Height: 1–7' **Spread:** 12–18"

Cuphea
Cuphea

C. hyssopifolia 'Allyson' (above), C. llavea (below)

Cupheas are wonderful plants for attracting hummingbirds and butterflies to your garden.

Cupheas are gaining in popularity. Their colorful and unusual flowers are sure to attract attention.

Growing
Cupheas prefer **full sun to partial shade,** in **moderately fertile, well-drained** soil. They do best with regular water but can handle short periods of dryness. Plant out after the risk of frost has passed.

Tips
Cupheas are excellent plants for containers of all descriptions, making it easy to bring them into the house, in a sunny window, for winter. They are also effective in an annual or mixed border and as edging.

Recommended
C. hyssopifolia (Mexican heather) is a bushy, many-branched plant that forms a flat-topped mound 12–24" tall and wide. A **Plant of Merit** selection, it produces light purple, pink or white flowers from summer to fall frost.

C. ignea (*C. platycentra;* cigar flower, firecracker plant) is a spreading, freely branching plant, 12–24" tall and 12–36" wide, that bears thin, tubular, bright red flowers from late spring to fall frost.

C. llavea (bat face, tiny mice) is a heat-tolerant, mounding to spreading plant, 12–18" tall and 12–24" wide, that produces an abundance of flowers with green to violet calyces and bright red petals.

Features: red, pink, purple, violet, green or white flowers; attractive growth habit
Height: 6–24" **Spread:** 10–36"

Dahlberg Daisy
Thymophylla

This delightful little flower is a favorite with novice gardeners. Its adaptability to poor, sandy soils makes it perfect for a rock garden or for growing in less-than-ideal environments.

Growing
Dahlberg daisy prefers **full sun,** in **well-drained** soil of **poor to average fertility,** but any well-drained soil is suitable. It prefers cool summers. In hot climates, it flowers in spring.

Direct-sown plants may not flower until quite late in summer. For earlier blooms, start the seeds indoors. Don't cover the seeds; they require light to germinate. Dahlberg daisy may self-sow and reappear each year.

To encourage new growth and more blooms, trim your plants back when flowering seems to be slowing, particularly when the weather cools.

Tips
Dahlberg daisy looks wonderful in any location where it can cascade over and trail down an edge. Use along the edges of borders, along the tops of rock walls or in hanging baskets or mixed containers.

Recommended
*T. **tenuiloba*** (Dyssodia tenuiloba) forms a mound of ferny foliage. From spring until the summer heat causes it to fade, it produces many daisy-like, bright yellow flowers. It is a **Plant of Merit.**

T. tenuiloba (above & below)

The cheerful Dahlberg daisy rarely suffers from pest or disease problems.

Also called: golden fleece **Features:** bright yellow or, less commonly, orange flowers; fragrant foliage; easy to grow
Height: 6–12" **Spread:** 12"

Fan Flower
Scaevola

S. aemula (above & below)

Given the right conditions, this Australian plant flowers abundantly from April through to fall frost.

Fan flower's intriguing one-sided flowers add interest to hanging baskets, planters and window boxes.

Growing
Fan flower grows well in **full sun** or **light shade**. The soil should be of **average fertility, moist** and very **well drained**. Water regularly because this plant doesn't like to dry out completely. It does, however, recover quickly from wilting when watered. Maintain a relatively frequent feeding schedule with a balanced fertilizer that includes micronutrients and iron.

Tips
Fan flower is popular for hanging baskets and containers, but it can also be used along the tops of rock walls and in rock gardens where it can trail down. This plant makes an interesting addition to mixed borders, or it can be used under shrubs where the long, trailing stems form an attractive groundcover.

Recommended
S. aemula forms a mound of foliage from which trailing stems emerge. The fan-shaped flowers come in shades of purple, usually with white bases. The species is rarely grown because the many improved cultivars are preferred. **'Blue Wonder'** is a **Plant of Merit** selection that has long, trailing branches, making it ideal for hanging baskets. It can eventually spread 36" or more.

Features: uniquely shaped, blue or purple flowers; trailing habit
Height: 8" **Spread:** up to 36" or more

Geranium
Pelargonium

Geraniums deserve a place in the annual garden. These colorful plants are tough, drought-resistant and dependable. For something out of the ordinary, seek out the scented geraniums with their fragrant and often decorative foliage.

Growing

Geraniums prefer **full sun** but tolerate partial shade, although they may not bloom as profusely. The soil should be **fertile** and **well drained**. Deadheading is essential to keep geraniums blooming and looking neat.

Tips

Geraniums are very popular for borders, beds, planters, hanging baskets and window boxes. Because they are perennials that are treated as annuals, they can be kept indoors over winter in a bright room.

Recommended

P. x *hortorum* (zonal geranium) is a bushy plant with red, pink, purple, orange or white flowers and, frequently, banded or multi-colored foliage. Many cultivars are available.

P. peltatum (ivy-leaved geranium) has thick, waxy leaves and a trailing habit. Many cultivars are available.

P. **species** and **cultivars** (scented geraniums) comprise a large group of geraniums that have scented leaves. The scents are grouped into the categories of rose, mint, citrus, fruit, spice and pungent.

P. x *hortorum* Fireworks Collection (above)
P. peltatum (below)

Visit a plant trial facility and see how many Pelargonium varieties are being tested and compared. You will discover that it is always possible to improve on a good plant.

Features: red, pink, violet, orange, salmon, white or purple flowers; decorative or scented foliage; variable habits
Height: 8–24" **Spread:** 6"–4'

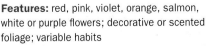

Globe Amaranth
Gomphrena

G. *globosa* (above & below)

Growing

Globe amaranth prefers **full sun, in well-drained** soil of **average fertility**. Provide adequate moisture when the plants are young, and water them during periods of extended drought. Established plants tolerate drought and heat. Deadhead to keep the plants tidy.

Soak the seeds in water for two to four days to encourage sprouting before sowing into warm soil (above 70° F). Seed sown in midsummer produces a colorful fall show.

Tips

Globe amaranth can be included in informal and cottage-style gardens as well as mixed beds and borders.

Globe amaranth flowers are popular for cutting and drying. Harvest the blooms when they become round and plump; dry them upside down in a cool, dry location.

G lobe amaranths are wonderful annuals for our hot summers. With the range in flower colors and plant sizes, there is a globe amaranth for every sunny, well-drained spot. Butterflies adore globe amaranths.

Globe amaranth flowerheads consist of brightly colored, papery bracts from which the tiny flowers emerge.

Recommended

G. globosa forms a rounded, bushy plant that bears papery, clover-like flowers in shades of purple, magenta, white or pink. Many cultivars are available, including more compact selections. **Buddy Series** plants are compact, growing 6–10" tall, and produce flowers in shades of white, purple and rose. 'Buddy Purple' has intense, deep purple flowers and is a **Plant of Merit**.

Features: purple, magenta, pink, white or red flowers; easy to grow; tough as nails
Height: 6–30" **Spread:** 6–15"

Impatiens
Impatiens

I. walleriana (above), *I. hawkeri* (below)

With their reliable blooming in shade and their wide variety of colors and types, impatiens are among America's top-selling bedding plants.

Growing

Impatiens do best in **partial shade** or **light shade,** but they tolerate full shade; if kept moist, some selections tolerate full sun. The soil should be **fertile, humus rich, moist** and **well drained**. New Guinea impatiens do not like wet feet, so good drainage is a must.

Tips

Impatiens grow and flower profusely even in shade. Mass plant them in beds under trees, along shady fences or walls or in porch planters. They also look lovely in hanging baskets.

Recommended

I. hawkeri (New Guinea hybrids; New Guinea impatiens) flowers in shades of red, orange, pink, purple or white. The foliage is often variegated, with a yellow stripe down the center of each leaf. This species can take more sun than *I. walleriana.*

I. walleriana (impatiens, busy Lizzie) flowers in shades of purple, red, burgundy, pink, yellow, salmon, orange, apricot or white and can be bicolored. Hundreds of cultivars are available.

Impatiens are self-grooming, meaning that they drop their spent blossoms on their own.

Features: colorful flowers in shades of purple, red, burgundy, pink, yellow, salmon, orange, apricot, white or bicolored; grows well in shade
Height: 6–36" **Spread:** 8–24"

Madagascar Periwinkle
Catharanthus

C. roseus (above & below)

Madagascar periwinkle is one of the best annuals to use in tough, urban settings. It has amazing heat tolerance and drought tolerance and cheerfully blooms amongst the exhaust fumes and dust of the city.

Growing

Madagascar periwinkle prefers **full sun** but tolerates partial shade. Any **well-drained** soil is fine. This plant tolerates pollution and drought, but it prefers to be watered regularly. It doesn't like to be too wet or too cold. Plant out after the soil has warmed.

Tips

Madagascar periwinkle does well in the sunniest, warmest part of the garden. Plant it in a bed along an exposed driveway or against the south-facing wall of the house. It can also be used in hanging baskets, in planters or as a temporary groundcover.

Recommended

C. roseus (*Vinca rosea*) forms a mound of strong stems. The flowers are pink, red or white, often with contrasting centers. Many cultivars are available.

A perennial grown as an annual, Madagascar periwinkle can be grown as a houseplant in a bright room.

Also called: vinca rosea **Features:** attractive foliage; red, rose, pink, mauve or white flowers, often with contrasting centers; durable **Height:** 10–24" **Spread:** usually equal to or greater than height

Marigold
Tagets

The warm colors and unique aroma of marigolds add a joyful air to the garden. There are a huge number to choose from, but one thing has remained constant: marigolds are easy to grow, withstand heat and tolerate dry conditions.

Growing

Marigolds grow best in **full sun,** in **well-drained** soil of **average fertility**. These plants tolerate drought and hold up well in windy, rainy weather. Deadhead to prolong blooming and to keep the plants tidy. *T. erecta* definitely needs to be deadheaded so the fading flowers don't decay and set off a gray mold infection.

Tips

Mass planted or mixed with other plants, marigolds make a vibrant addition to beds, borders and container gardens. These plants thrive in the hottest, driest parts of your garden.

Recommended

Many cultivars are available for all the species. *T. erecta* (African marigold, American marigold, Aztec marigold) offers the largest plants with the biggest flowers. *T. patula* (French marigold) is low growing and has a wide range of flower colors. *T.* **Triploid Hybrids** (triploid marigold) have been developed by crossing French and African marigolds, which results in plants with huge flowers and compact growth.

T. patula 'Boy Series' (above)
T. patula hybrid (below)

Features: bright yellow, red, orange, brown, gold, cream or bicolored flowers; fragrant foliage; easy to grow
Height: 6–36" **Spread:** 12–24"

Million Bells

Calibrachoa

C. Million Bells Series TERRA COTTA (above)
C. Superbells Series 'Trailing Pink' (below)

Million bells blooms well into fall; the flowers become hardier as the weather cools, and your plants may survive temperatures down to 20° F.

Million bells is extremely floriferous. This low-growing, compact, vigorous plant tolerates our summer heat and requires no dead-heading. Feed it often, especially when growing it in hanging baskets and planters.

Growing

Million bells prefers **full sun**. The soil should be **fertile, moist** and **well drained**. Although it prefers to be watered regularly, million bells is fairly drought resistant once established.

Tips

Popular for planters and hanging baskets, million bells is also attractive in beds and borders. It grows all summer and needs plenty of room to spread, or it will overtake other flowers. Pinch back to keep the plants compact.

Recommended

C. Hybrids have a dense, trailing habit. They bear small flowers that look like petunias. The **Million Bells Series** includes upright and trailing plants bearing yellow, orange, brick red, dark blue, purple, pink or bright yellow flowers with yellow centers. TERRA COTTA ('Sunbelkist') is a **Plant of Merit**. The **Superbells Series** is noted for superior disease resistance and a wide range of uniquely colored flowers.

Also called: trailing petunia **Features:** pink, purple, yellow, brick red, orange, white or blue flowers; trailing or erect habit
Height: 6–12" **Spread:** up to 24"

Nicotiana
Nicotiana

Gardeners have long appreciated the many positive qualities of nicotianas, including the wonderful aroma of the flowers. The fragrance, in some cases, has been lost in favor of an expanded selection of flower colors.

Growing
Nicotianas grow well in **full sun, light shade** or **partial shade,** although the plants appreciate some shade from the hot afternoon sun. The soil should be **fertile, high in organic matter, moist** and **well drained**.

Tips
Nicotianas are popular in beds and borders. The dwarf varieties do well in containers. Tall plants may need staking. Sow seed indoors early or sow directly into warm soil.

Do not plant nicotianas near tomatoes, eggplants, potatoes or peppers. They are all from the same plant family and share a vulnerability to many of the same diseases. Nicotianas may attract and harbor diseases that hardly affect it but that can kill tomatoes.

Recommended
N. alata is an upright plant that grows up to 5' tall and has a strong, sweet fragrance.

N. **Hummingbird Series** offers compact plants with fragrant flowers available in red, pink, lilac, green and white. This series is excellent at the front of a border or massed.

N. sylvestris and *N.* x *sanderae* Nicki Series (above)
N. x *sanderae* Nicki Series (below)

N. **x** *sanderae* is a hybrid from which many brightly colored and dwarf cultivars have been developed.

N. **sylvestris** bears white blooms that are fragrant in the evening. It is an **Emeritus Plant of Merit**.

Also called: flowering tobacco
Features: red, pink, green, yellow, white or purple flowers, some with fragrance; bold foliage
Height: 6"–5' **Spread:** 10–24"

Nierembergia
Nierembergia

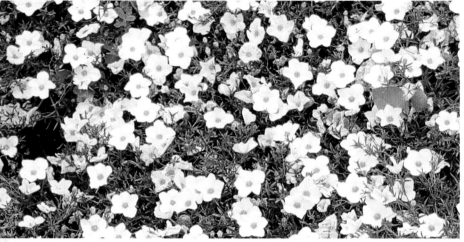

N. hippomanica 'Mont Blanc' (above), *N. scoparia* 'Purple Robe' (below)

The flowers of nierembergias float like stars atop fern-like foliage. These plants are lovely for planting under roses and other flowering shrubs.

Growing

Nierembergias grow well in **full sun** or **partial shade**. They do best in the cooler part of the garden, with protection from the afternoon sun. The soil should be of **average fertility, moist** and **well drained**.

The species names in the genus Nierembergia are confused. The recommended selections may be listed as belonging to one of the following species: N. caerulea, N. frutescens, N. hippomanica or N. scoparia.

Nierembergias are perennials used as annuals. If your plants survive winter, take it as a bonus. However, it is often easier to start new plants each year than to overwinter mature plants.

Tips

Use nierembergias as groundcover, for edging beds and borders or for rock gardens, rock walls, containers and hanging baskets. They grow best when summers are cool, and they can withstand a light frost.

Recommended

N. hippomanica '**Mont Blanc**' (*N. scoparia* 'Mont Blanc') is a **Plant of Merit** that forms a small mound of foliage and bears delicate, cup-shaped, white flowers with yellow centers.

N. scoparia '**Purple Robe**' is a dense, compact, mat-forming perennial that bears deep purple flowers with golden eyes. It is a **Plant of Merit**.

Features: purple or white flowers; habit; foliage
Height: 6–12" **Spread:** 6–12"

Persian Shield
Strobilanthes

The intense, iridescent foliage of Persian shield adds an unusual and striking look to containers, baskets or any annual or mixed planting.

Growing
Persian shield grows well in **full sun** or **partial shade**. The soil should be **average to fertile, light** and very **well drained**. Pinch the growing tips to encourage bushy growth. Cuttings can be started in late summer and overwintered indoors.

Tips
The colorful foliage provides a dramatic background in annual or mixed beds and borders and in container plantings. For stunning contrast, combine Persian shield with plants that bear yellow, white, red or purple flowers or with plants such as the lime green 'Margarita' Sweet Potato Vine (*Ipomoea batatas* 'Margarita'). Persian shield works well as a groundcover. The flowers are insignificant and often don't form before the first fall frost.

Recommended
S. dyerianus is a tender shrub that is grown as an annual. It forms a mound of silver- or purple-flushed foliage with contrasting dark green, bronze or purple veins and margins. Although it happens rarely in Missouri, spikes of blue flowers may appear in early fall. Persian shield is a **Plant of Merit**.

S. dyerianus (above & below)

The common name of this plant arose because its foliage was thought to resemble the colorful shields carried by soldiers in ancient Persia.

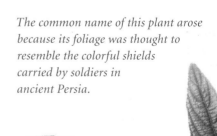

Features: decorative foliage
Height: 18–36" **Spread:** 24–36" or more

Petunia

Petunia

P. 'Purple Wave' (above), *P.* multiflora type (below)

Petunias are beautiful flowers that can be enjoyed all summer long.

For speedy growth, prolific blooming and ease of care, petunias are hard to beat. Even the most neglected plants continue to bloom all summer.

Growing

Petunias prefer **full sun**. The soil should be of **average to rich fertility, light, sandy** and **well drained**. Pinch halfway back in mid-summer to keep the plants bushy and to encourage new growth and flowers.

Most recently released varieties do not require the excessive deadheading that previously made the maintenance of petunias a chore, although thorough deadheading at least once a week remains a good idea.

Tips

Use petunias in beds, borders, containers and hanging baskets.

Recommended

P. **x** *hybrida* is a large group of popular, sun-loving annuals that fall into three categories. **Grandifloras** have the largest flowers in the widest range of colors, but they can be damaged by rain. **Millifloras** have the smallest flowers in the narrowest range of colors, but this type is the most prolific and the least likely to be damaged by heavy rain. **Multifloras,** including **Wave Series** plants, have smaller and more flowers than the grandifloras, and they tolerate adverse weather conditions better.

Features: pink, purple, red, white, yellow, coral, blue or bicolored flowers; versatility
Height: 6–18" **Spread:** 12–24" or wider

Portulaca

Portulaca

For a brilliant show in the hottest, driest, most neglected area of the garden, you can't go wrong with portulaca.

Growing

Portulaca requires **full sun**. The soil should be of **poor fertility, sandy** and **well drained**. If you sow directly outdoors, rain may transport the tiny seeds to unexpected places. To ensure that you have the plants where you want them, start the seed indoors.

Tips

Portulaca is the ideal plant for garden spots that just don't get enough water—under the eaves of the house or in dry, rocky, exposed areas. It is also ideal for people who like baskets hanging from the front porch but who forget to water them. As long as the location is sunny, this plant does well with minimal care.

P. grandiflora (above & below)

Recommended

P. grandiflora forms a bushy mound of succulent foliage. It bears delicate, papery, rose-like flowers profusely all summer. Many cultivars are available, including ones with flowers that stay open on cloudy days.

Spacing portulacas closely together is not a problem; rather, the intertwining of the plants and colorful flowers creates an interesting and attractive effect.

Also called: moss rose
Features: red, pink, yellow, white, purple, orange or peach flowers; drought resistant; interesting foliage; easy to grow
Height: 4–8" **Spread:** 6–12" or wider

Salvia

Salvia

S. splendens (above), S. farinacea 'Victoria' (below)

There are over 900 species of Salvia, including culinary sage and many perennial flower species.

Salvias should be part of every annual garden. Their attractive and varied forms have something to offer every style of garden, from cottage to formal.

Growing

All salvias prefer **full sun** but tolerate light shade. The soil should be **moist** and **well drained, high in organic matter** and of **average to rich fertility**.

Tips

Salvias look good grouped in beds and borders or in containers. The long-lasting flowers are good for cut-flower arrangements.

To keep the plants producing flowers, water often and fertilize monthly. Remove spent flowers before they begin to turn brown.

Recommended

S. coccinea (Texas sage) is a bushy, upright plant that bears whorled spikes of white, pink, blue or purple flowers.

S. farinacea (mealy cup sage, blue sage) has bright blue flowers clustered along stems powdered with silver. Cultivars are available.

S. splendens (salvia, scarlet sage) is grown for its spikes of tubular, bright red flowers. Recent cultivars also offer white, pink, purple or orange flowers.

Also called: sage
Features: red, blue, purple, burgundy, pink, orange, salmon, yellow, cream, white or bicolored summer flowers; attractive foliage
Height: 1–4' **Spread:** 8"–4'

Sweet Alyssum
Lobularia

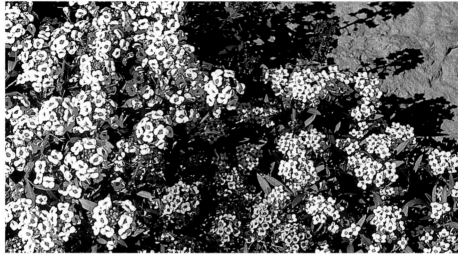

L. maritima cultivars (above & below)

Sweet alyssum makes a lovely carpet of blooms to weave through formal and informal plantings. It is excellent for creating soft edges in beds and borders and along pathways.

Growing

Sweet alyssum prefers **full sun** but tolerates light shade. **Well-drained** soil of **average fertility** is preferred, but poor soil is tolerated. Sweet alyssum may die back a bit during the heat and humidity of summer. Trim it back and water it periodically to encourage new growth and more flowers when the weather cools.

Leave alyssum plants out all winter. In spring, remove the previous year's growth to expose the self-sown seedlings below.

Tips

Sweet alyssum creeps around rock gardens, over rock walls and along the edges of beds. It is an excellent choice for seeding into cracks and crevices of walkways and between patio stones. Once established, it readily reseeds. It is also good for filling in spaces between taller plants in borders and mixed containers.

Recommended

L. maritima forms a low, spreading mound of foliage. The entire plant appears to be covered in tiny blossoms when in full flower. Cultivars with flowers in a wide range of colors are available. **'Snow Crystals'** has large, fragrant flowers and is an **Emeritus Plant of Merit**.

Features: fragrant, pink, purple, yellow, salmon or white flowers
Height: 3–12" **Spread:** 6–24"

Sweet Potato Vine

Ipomoea

I. batatas 'Margarita' (above & below)

If you haven't tried it yet, grow sweet potato vine. This vigorous, rambling plant with leaves of lime green, bruise purple or a variegated green, pink and cream can make any gardener look like a genius.

Growing

Grow sweet potato vine in **full sun**. Any type of soil will do, but a **light, well-drained** soil of **poor fertility** is preferred.

As a bonus, when you pull up your sweet potato vine at the end of summer, you can eat any tubers (sweet potatoes) that have formed.

Tips

Sweet potato vine is a great addition to mixed planters, window boxes and hanging baskets. It scrambles about in a rock garden and cascades over the edge when planted at the top of a retaining wall.

Recommended

I. batatas is a twining climber that is grown for its attractive foliage rather than its flowers. Several cultivars are available. **'Black Heart'** has heart-shaped, dark purple-green foliage with darker veins. **'Blackie'** has deeply lobed, dark purple leaves. **'Margarita'** has heart-shaped, yellow-green foliage. **'Tricolor'** has variegated foliage in pink, green and white.

Features: decorative foliage
Height: about 12" **Spread:** up to 10'

Verbena

Verbena

These annuals demand dry, well-drained soil, so they are best grown on sunny mounds, along raised median strips and with plants that suck moisture out of the soil, such as junipers.

Growing

Verbenas grow best in **full sun**. The soil should be **fertile** and very **well drained**. Pinch back the young plants for bushy growth.

Tips

Use verbenas on rock walls and in beds, borders, rock gardens, containers, hanging baskets and window boxes. They make good substitutes for ivy-leaved geraniums where the sun is hot and where a roof overhang keeps the mildew-prone verbenas dry.

Recommended

V. bonariensis forms a low clump of foliage from which tall, stiff stems emerge, bearing clusters of small, purple flowers. Butterflies love this **Plant of Merit** selection.

V. canadensis is a low-growing, spreading plant that bears clusters of pink flowers from mid-summer to fall. 'Homestead Purple' bears dark purple flowers and is mildew resistant.

V. x hybrida is a bushy plant that may be upright or spreading. It bears clusters of small flowers in a wide range of colors. Cultivars are available. '**Imagination**' is a compact plant and is another **Plant of Merit**. It tolerates heat and drought, and

V. bonariensis (above), *V. x hybrida* (below)

it has intense violet-blue flowers that bloom over a long period from May to the first hard frost.

V. pendula **Superbena Series** is vigorous, upright to trailing plants with excellent mildew resistance. The large flowers bloom in intense shades of red, pink and purple.

Also called: garden verbena **Features:** red, pink, purple, purple-blue, blue, salmon, yellow, scarlet, burgundy or white flowers that bloom in summer, some with white centers
Height: 4"–5' **Spread:** 10–36"

Viola
Viola

V. x wittrockiana (above), *V. tricolor* (below)

Violas are a cottage garden staple. Two of the most popular species—pansies and Johnny-jump-ups—reseed and create a dazzling display in odd places such as gravel driveways, between evergreen shrubs and in the cracks of sidewalks.

The more flowers you pick, the more profusely violas bloom.

Growing

Violas prefer **full sun** but tolerate partial shade. The soil should be **fertile, moist** and **well drained**. Violas do best in cool weather, and they may die back completely in the summer heat.

Tips

Violas can be used in beds, borders or containers—or mix them with spring-flowering bulbs. The varied color combinations of pansies complement almost every other type of bedding plant.

Plant more violas in late summer and early fall to refresh tired and faded flowerbeds. Violas often reawaken in spring if left to go dormant in fall, allowing for early-spring flowers. In warm areas of the state, some pansies bloom throughout mild winters.

Recommended

V. tricolor (Johnny-jump-up) has purple, white and yellow flower colors, usually in combination. Several varieties have flowers in a single color, often purple. This plant thrives in gravel.

V. x wittrockiana (pansy) is available in a wide variety of solid, patterned, bicolored or multi-colored flowers, with face-like markings in every size imaginable.

Features: blue, purple, red, orange, yellow, pink, white or multi-colored flowers; easy to grow; low maintenance
Height: 3–10" **Spread:** 4–12"

Zinnia
Zinnia

Zinnias have a wide range of uses in both formal and informal gardens and also in containers. They are outstanding in cut-flower gardens.

Growing
Zinnias grow best in **full sun**. The soil should be **fertile, rich in organic matter, moist** and **well drained**. To avoid disturbing the roots when transplanting seedlings, start the seeds in individual peat pots. Deadhead to prolong blooming and to keep the plants looking neat.

Tips
Zinnias are useful in beds, borders, containers and cutting gardens. The dwarf selections can be used as edging plants. These plants provide wonderful fall color.

Recommended
Z. angustifolia **'Classic'** (Mexican zinnia) is a bushy plant, 8–12" tall and wide, which bears bright, daisy-like flowers in shades of orange, yellow, gold or white. This **Emeritus Plant of Merit** selection is drought and disease tolerant.

Z. elegans is a bushy, upright plant with daisy-like flowers in a variety of forms. Heights vary from 6–36". Many cultivars are available.

Z. Profusion Series offers fast-growing, mildew-resistant, compact hybrids. These All-America Selections winners bear bright cherry red, orange or white flowers.

Z. angustifolia 'Classic' (above), *Z. elegans* (below)

Mildew can be a problem for zinnias, so choose mildew-resistant cultivars, grow them in locations with good air circulation and avoid wetting the foliage

Features: bushy plants; colorful flowers in shades of red, yellow, green, purple, orange, pink, white, maroon, brown or gold, with some bicolored or tricolored
Height: 6–36" **Spread:** 8–12"

Aster

Aster

A. novae-angliae (above), A. novi-belgii (below)

Purple and pink asters make a nice contrast to the yellow-flowered perennials that bloom in late summer. You will also have birds, butterflies and bees arriving for a late-summer or fall feed.

Growing

Asters prefer **full sun** but benefit from some afternoon shade to keep them from suffering in August's heat and humidity. The soil should be **fertile, moist** and **well drained**.

Pinch or shear these plants back in early summer to promote dense growth and reduce disease problems. Mulch in winter to protect the plants from temperature fluctuations. Divide every two or three years to maintain vigor and control spread.

Tips

Use asters in the middle to back of borders and in cottage gardens, or naturalize them in wild gardens.

Recommended

Some aster species have recently been reclassified under the genus names *Symphyotrichum* and *Eurybia*. You may encounter these names at garden centers.

A. novae-angliae (Michaelmas daisy, New England aster) is an upright, spreading, clump-forming perennial that bears yellow-centered, purple flowers. Many cultivars are available.

A. novi-belgii (Michaelmas daisy, New York aster) is a dense, upright, clump-forming perennial with purple flowers. Many cultivars are available.

A. oblongifolius (aromatic aster) is a mound-forming, bushy **Plant of Merit** that spreads by rhizomes and bears yellow-centered, violet-purple flowers. The foliage emits a spicy to pine-like aroma when bruised or crushed. This plant is hardy only to zone 5.

Among the final plants to bloom before the snow flies, asters often provide a last meal for migrating butterflies.

Features: red, white, blue, purple or pink late summer to mid-fall flowers, often with yellow centers **Height:** 7"–5' **Spread:** 18–36" **Hardiness:** zones 3–8

Astilbe

Astilbe

*T*he name "astilbe" come from the Greek language and translates as "without brilliance"—a rather unfitting name for this wonderful shade garden beauty.

Growing

Astilbes grow best in **light or partial shade** and tolerate full shade, although they do not flower as much in full shade. The soil should be **fertile, humus rich, acidic, moist** and **well drained**. Although they appreciate moist soil, astilbes don't like standing water. Use mulch in summer to keep the roots cool and moist.

Divide astilbes every three years or so to maintain plant vigor. If the root masses lift out of the soil as the plants mature, just add a layer of topsoil and mulch or replant them deeper.

Tips

Astilbes can be grown near the edges of bog gardens and ponds and in woodland gardens and shaded borders.

Recommended

A. **x** *arendsii* (false spirea, Arend's astilbe) is a group of hybrids with many available cultivars.

A. chinensis (Chinese astilbe) is a dense, vigorous perennial that tolerates dry soil better than other astilbe species. **Var. pumila** is a low-growing **Plant of Merit** selection that bears dark pink flowers.

A. x *arendsii* cultivars (above)
A. x *arendsii* 'Bressingham Beauty' (below)

A. simplicifolia **'Sprite'** (star astilbe) is an upright variety that forms spreading clumps. It produces silvery pink blooms and rich green foliage.

Astilbes self-seed easily, and the flowerheads provide interest well into fall. Deadheading does not extend the blooming period, so the choice is yours whether to remove the spent blossoms.

Features: attractive foliage; white, pink, purple, peach or red summer flowers **Height:** 1–5'
Spread: 18–36" **Hardiness:** zones 3–9

Black-Eyed Susan

Rudbeckia

R. fulgida with purple coneflower (above)

Growing

Black-eyed Susans grow well in **full sun** or **partial shade**. The soil should be of **average fertility** and **well drained**. Several *Rudbeckia* species that tolerate fairly heavy clay soils are touted as "claybusters." Established plants tolerate drought, but regular watering is best. Divide in spring or fall every three to five years.

Tips

Plant black-eyed Susans wherever you want a casual look. They look great planted in drifts. Include these native plants in wildflower and natural gardens, beds and borders. Pinching the plants in June results in shorter, bushier stands.

Recommended

R. fulgida is an upright, spreading plant, 24–36" tall, that bears orange-yellow flowers with brown centers. **Var. *sullivantii* 'Goldsturm'** bears large, bright golden yellow flowers.

R. laciniata (cutleaf coneflower) forms a large, open clump. It grows 4–9' tall and bears yellow flowers with green centers.

R. missouriensis (Missouri coneflower) grows 24–36" tall and has black-centered, orange to yellow flowers. It spreads to form colonies.

Perennial black-eyed Susans are tough, low maintenance and long-lived. They are excellent for a casual-looking garden. Black-eyed Susans look great planted in drifts.

Black-eyed Susans last well when cut for arrangements.

Features: bright yellow, orange or red flowers with brown, green or black centers from midsummer to fall; attractive foliage; easy to grow
Height: 18"–9' **Spread:** 12–36"
Hardiness: zones 3–9

Bluestar

Amsonia

Bluestars are great three-season plants that provide cool spring flowers, attractive summer foliage and wonderful fall color. Use them either integrated at the back of a perennial bed or by themselves as specimens.

Growing

Plant bluestars in **full sun** to **partial shade,** in **well-drained** soil of **moderate fertility.** Too rich a soil results in thin, open growth and not as many flowers. *A. tabernaemontana* tolerates drought once established. To propagate more plants, divide bluestars in spring or sow seed.

Tips

These pretty plants have a fine, billowy appearance. Plant them in groups of three to five to achieve the most stunning results.

The willow-like foliage of bluestars turns an attractive yellow in fall, and their love of moist soil makes them a beautiful addition alongside a stream or pond, as well as in a border.

Recommended

A. **hubrichtii** forms a small, delicate shrub with clusters of sky blue blooms in spring. It prefers a moist soil. This **Plant of Merit** has narrow, feathery leaves that turn golden yellow in fall.

A. hubrichtii (above & below)

A. **tabernaemontana** is a Missouri native and a **Plant of Merit** selection that produces small, lavender blue flowers. **Var.** *salicifolia* has narrower leaves and more open clusters of flowers than the species.

Be sure to wash your hands thoroughly after handling bluestars because some people find the sap irritates their skin.

Also called: willow bluestar **Features:** blue flowers from spring through summer; attractive growth habit and foliage **Height:** 15"–4' **Spread:** 2–5' **Hardiness:** zones 3–9

Boltonia

Boltonia

B. asteroides (above & below)

Less susceptible to powdery mildew, boltonia is a good alternative to the tall asters.

Boltonia is a tall, easy-to-grow, pest- and disease-free plant that blooms profusely for four weeks or more, and it brings fresh color to the garden late in the season.

Growing

Boltonia prefers **full sun** and **fertile, humus rich, moist, well-drained** soil. It tolerates partial shade and adapts to less fertile soils, and it even tolerates some drought. Divide in fall or early spring, when the clump is overgrown or dying out in the middle.

The stout stems rarely require staking. If your plants grow too tall for your liking, cut the stems back by one-third in June.

Tips

This large plant can be used in the middle or at the back of a mixed border, in a naturalized or cottage-style garden or near a pond or other water feature.

Recommended

B. asteroides is a large, upright perennial with narrow, grayish green leaves. It bears a lot of daisy-like, white or slightly purple flowers with yellow centers. **'Pink Beauty'** has a looser habit and bears pale pink flowers. **'Snowbank'** is an **Emeritus Plant of Merit** with a denser, more compact habit and bears more plentiful white flowers than the species.

Features: white, mauve or pink, late summer and fall flowers with yellow centers; easy to grow
Height: 3–6' **Spread:** up to 4'
Hardiness: zones 4–9

Brunnera
Brunnera

These beautiful, shade-loving plants are a welcome addition to any garden. The variegated selections bring light to corners of the garden that might otherwise seem dark.

Growing

Brunnera grows best in **light shade,** but it will also grow in partial shade with morning sun if the soil is kept consistently moist; brunnera does not tolerate drought. The soil should be of **average fertility, humus rich, moist** and **well drained**. Cut back faded foliage in mid-summer to encourage a flush of new growth.

Tips

Brunnera makes a great addition to a woodland or shaded garden. Its low, bushy habit makes it useful as a groundcover or as an addition to a shaded border.

Recommended

B. macrophylla is an **Emeritus Plant of Merit** that forms a mound of soft, heart-shaped leaves and produces loose clusters of blue flowers all spring. Cultivars with silver- or cream-variegated foliage are available. **'Dawson's White'** ('Variegata') has large leaves with irregular creamy patches. **'Jack Frost'** bears silvery white foliage with green veins and a thin green margin. Grow variegated plants in light or full shade to avoid scorched leaves.

B. macrophylla 'Jack Frost' (above)
B. macrophylla 'Dawson's White' (below)

Brunnera, which is related to borage and forget-me-nots, rarely suffers from any problems.

Also called: Siberian bugloss **Features:** blue spring flowers; attractive foliage
Height: 12–18" **Spread:** 18–24"
Hardiness: zones 3–8

Butterfly Weed

Asclepias

A. tuberosa (above & below)

Butterfly weed, a North American native, will attract butterflies to your garden. It is a major food source for the monarch butterfly.

Growing

Butterfly weed prefers **full sun** and **well-drained** soil. *A. tuberosa* tolerates drought once established, but it enjoys some moisture in an extended drought. The deep taproot makes division very difficult. To propagate, use the seedlings that sprout up around the base of the plant. Deadhead to encourage a second blooming.

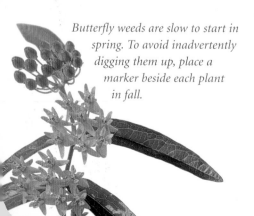

Butterfly weeds are slow to start in spring. To avoid inadvertently digging them up, place a marker beside each plant in fall.

Tips

Use *A. tuberosa* in meadow plantings and borders, on dry banks, in neglected areas and in wildflower, cottage and butterfly gardens. Use *A. incarnata* in moist borders and in bog, pondside or streamside plantings.

Recommended

A. incarnata (swamp milkweed) forms a dense clump of thick stems and bears clusters of pink, white or light purple flowers in late spring or early summer. Cultivars are available.

A. tuberosa (butterfly weed) forms a clump of leafy, upright stems. It bears clusters of orange flowers from mid-summer to early fall. Cultivars are available that bear scarlet, gold, orange, pink or bicolored flowers.

Also called: milkweed, pleurisy root
Features: red, yellow, orange, gold, white, pink, light purple or bicolored flowers; attracts butterflies **Height:** 18–36" **Spread:** 12–24"
Hardiness: zones 4–9

Cardinal Flower

Lobelia

*T*he brilliant red of the flowers is motivation enough for some gardeners to install a pond or bog garden just to meet the moist soil requirements of these plants.

Growing

Cardinal flowers grow well in **full sun, light shade** or **partial shade**. The soil should be **fertile, slightly acidic** and **moist**. Ensure the soil remains moist, especially in full sun. Mulch the plants for winter protection. Deadhead to keep the plants neat and to encourage a possible second flush of blooms. The plants tend to self-seed, and seedlings can be moved to new locations or left in place to replace their short-lived parents.

Tips

These plants are best suited to streamsides, pondsides or bog gardens, but they can also be used in beds and borders that are watered regularly.

Recommended

L. cardinalis (cardinal flower) is a Missouri native and a **Plant of Merit** selection that forms an erect clump of bronze-green leaves and bears spikes of bright red flowers from summer to fall.

L. siphilitica (blue cardinal flower) forms an erect clump with bright green foliage. Spikes of deep blue flowers appear from mid-summer to fall.

L. x speciosa is the hardiest, most vigorous of the cardinal flowers, with blooms in shades of blue, purple, red or pink.

L. cardinalis (above & below)

Cardinal flowers contain deadly alkaloids and have poisoned people who tried to use them in herbal medicines.

Features: bright red, purple, blue or pink summer flowers; bronze-green foliage
Height: 2–4' **Spread:** 12–24"
Hardiness: zones 4–9

Catmint

Nepeta

N. x faassenii 'Walker's Low' (above), *N. x faassenii* (below)

Catmint is a member of the mint family. This real workhorse of the garden bed offers season-long blooms on sturdy, fragrant, trouble-free plants.

Growing

Catmint grows well in **full sun** or **partial shade**. The soil should be of **average fertility** and **well drained**. Catmint tends to flop over in fertile soil. Pinch the plants back in early June to encourage bushy, compact growth. Cut back after blooming to encourage a second flush of flowers.

Cats are strongly attracted to catnip (N. cataria), *and you may find that cats are also drawn to your garden if you grow catmint.*

Tips

The low-growing catmints can be used to edge borders and pathways or in rock gardens. Tall selections make lovely additions to perennial beds. All catmints work well in herb gardens and with roses in cottage gardens.

Recommended

N. **x** *faassenii* forms a clump of spreading, upright stems. Spikes of blue or lavender flowers are produced in spring and summer and sometimes again in fall. Many cultivars and hybrids are available. **'Blue Wonder'** grows 10–14" tall and 12–18" wide. This **Emeritus Plant of Merit** produces dense, gray-green foliage and dark blue flowers. **'Walker's Low'** has gray-green foliage and bears lavender blue flowers. It grows about 10" tall.

Features: blue, purple, pink or white spring or summer flowers; habit; fragrant foliage
Height: 10–36" **Spread:** 10–36"
Hardiness: zones 3–8

Coral Bells

Heuchera

Few perennials available to Missouri gardeners offer the tremendous variety of leaf sizes, shapes and colors as do coral bells.

Growing

Coral bells grow best in **light or partial shade** because the foliage colors can bleach out in full sun, and full shade produces leggy plants. The soil should be of **average to rich fertility, humus rich, neutral to alkaline, moist** and **well drained**. Good air circulation is essential.

Deadhead to prolong the blooming season. Dig the plants up every two or three years and remove the oldest, woodiest roots and stems. The plants may be divided at this time, then replanted with the crown at or just above soil level.

Tips

Use coral bells as edging plants, in clusters and woodland gardens or as groundcover in low-traffic areas. Combine different foliage types for an interesting display.

H. micrantha 'Chocolate Ruffles' (above)
H. sanguineum (below)

Recommended

The dozens of beautiful cultivars available offer almost limitless variations of foliage markings and colors. **H. micrantha 'Chocolate Ruffles'** is an **Emeritus Plant of Merit;** the ruffled, glossy, brown leaves have purple undersides that produce a bronzed appearance.

Coral bells have a strange habit of pushing themselves up out of the soil. Mulch the plants in fall if they begin heaving from the ground.

Also called: alum root **Features:** very decorative foliage; red, pink, white, yellow or purple flowers in spring or summer
Height: 1–4' **Spread:** 12–18"
Hardiness: zones 3–9

Daylily
Hemerocallis

H. 'Stella d'Oro' (above), H. 'Bonanza' (below)

Missouri has some challenging gardening conditions. Fortunately, we can count on durable and adaptable daylilies to provide us with variety in color, blooming period, size and texture year after year.

Growing

Daylilies grow in any light from **full sun to full shade,** but the deeper the shade, the fewer flowers are produced. The soil should be **fertile, moist** and **well drained**, but these plants adapt to most conditions and are hard to kill once established. For best flower display, feed in spring and mid-summer. Divide every two or three years to keep the plants vigorous and to propagate them. They can, however, be left indefinitely without dividing.

Tips

Plant daylilies alone or group them in borders, on banks and in ditches to control erosion. They can be naturalized in woodland or meadow gardens. Small varieties are nice in planters.

Deadhead to prolong the blooming period. Be careful when deadheading purple-flowered daylilies because the sap can stain fingers and clothes.

Recommended

Daylilies come in an almost infinite number of forms, sizes and colors, in a range of species, cultivars and hybrids. See your local garden center or daylily grower to find out what's available and most suitable for your garden. **'Stella d'Oro'** is a repeat bloomer. The bright golden yellow flowers are borne on modest-sized 12" plants.

Features: spring and summer flowers in every color except blue and pure white; grass-like foliage **Height:** 1–5' **Spread:** 2–4' or more **Hardiness:** zones 2–9

False Indigo
Baptisia

False indigo is another beautiful Missouri native that requires minimal care and provides years of enjoyment. Be patient, though, because young plants may take a few years to grow large enough to flower.

Growing

False indigo prefers **full sun** but tolerates partial shade; too much shade causes lank growth that flops over easily. The soil should be of **poor to average fertility, sandy** and **well drained**.

Tips

False indigo can be used in an informal border or a cottage-style garden. It is an attractive addition for a naturalized planting, on a slope or in any sunny, well-drained spot.

Recommended

B. australis is a Missouri native and a **Plant of Merit**. It is an upright or somewhat spreading, clump-forming plant that bears spikes of purple-blue flowers in early summer. The swollen seedpods provide interest in late summer and fall. **'Purple Smoke'** is a hybrid with *B. australis* as one of the parents. It has smoky purple-white flowers.

B. australis 'Purple Smoke' (above)
B. australis (below)

If you've had difficulties growing lupines, try the far less demanding false indigo instead.

Features: purple-blue or purple-white flowers in late spring or early summer; attractive habit and foliage; seedpods **Height:** 3–5'
Spread: 2–4' **Hardiness:** zones 3–8

False Sunflower
Heliopsis

H. helianthoides (above & below)

False sunflower is an excellent, dependable, long-lived perennial that produces a dazzling display of bright yellow flowers from late summer into fall.

The stiff stems of false sunflower make the blooms a useful addition to fresh arrangements.

Growing

False sunflower prefers **full sun** but tolerates partial shade. The soil should be **average to fertile, humus rich, moist** and **well drained**. Most soil conditions are tolerated, including poor, dry soils, but the plant is not drought tolerant over long periods. If grown in an overly rich soil or in partial shade, the plants may need staking during the first year.

Divide every two or so years. Deadhead to prolong the blooming period. Cut the plants back once flowering is complete.

Tips

Use false sunflower at the back or in the middle of perennial or mixed borders. This easy-to-grow plant is popular with novice gardeners.

Recommended

H. helianthoides forms an upright clump of stems and foliage. It bears daisy-like, yellow or orange flowers from mid-summer to mid-fall. The following cultivars grow to half the height of the species. **'Golden Plume'** has double, yellow flowers. **'Summer Sun'** ('Sommersonne') is a **Plant of Merit** that bears single or semi-double flowers in bright golden yellow.

Also called: ox eye, orange sunflower
Features: long-lived; bright yellow to orange flowers; dependable; easy to grow
Height: 3–6' **Spread:** 18"–4'
Hardiness: zones 2–9

Goldenrod

Solidago and Solidaster

*T*he cultivated goldenrod varieties have brought the disorderly and wild appearance of the species under control, without diminishing the proliferation of blooms.

Growing

Goldenrod prefers **full sun** and tolerates partial shade. The soil should be of **poor to average fertility, light** and **well drained**. Soil that is too fertile results in lush growth, few flowers and invasive behavior.

To keep the plants vigorous and to control growth, divide them every three to five years in spring or fall.

Tips

Goldenrod plants are great for providing late-season color. They look at home in a large border, cottage garden or wildflower garden. Don't plant them near less vigorous plants because goldenrod can quickly overwhelm them. Goldenrod is great for xeriscaping.

Recommended

Solidago **hybrids** form a clump of strong stems with narrow leaves. They grow about 2–4' tall and spread about 18–24" wide. Plume-like clusters of yellow flowers are produced from mid-summer to fall. **'Golden Shower'** bears flowers in horizontal or drooping plumes.

S. sphacelata **'Golden Fleece'** is a mound-forming, branched perennial that grows 18–24" tall and wide. This **Plant of Merit** bears long, arching, spike-like clusters of bright golden yellow flowers.

S. hybrid (above & below)

x *Solidaster luteus* is a 24–30" tall and wide hybrid genus of a *Solidago* species and an *Aster* species. It bears daisy-like, pale yellow flowers with darker yellow centers.

Ragweeds (Ambrosia species), not goldenrods, are the source of hay-fever pollen.

Features: yellow flowers from mid-summer through fall; growth habit **Height:** 18"–4'
Spread: 18–30" **Hardiness:** zones 3–8

Hellebore

Helleborus

H. orientalis cultivar (above), *H. foetidus* (below)

Growing

Hellebores prefer **light, dappled shade** in a **sheltered** site. The soil should be **fertile, moist, humus rich, neutral to alkaline** and **well drained**. Protect the plants with mulch in winter. In mild winters, the flowers may poke up through the snow.

Hellebores don't divide well. Moving seedlings is an easier method to increase plant numbers. Trim back the leaves in spring for fresh growth. The leathery foliage has sharp leaf edges, so wear gloves and long sleeves when handling these plants.

Tips

Use these plants in a sheltered border or rock garden or allow them to naturalize in a woodland garden.

Recommended

H. foetidus (bear's-foot hellebore, stinking hellebore) grows 30" tall and wide and bears dark green leaves and clusters of light green flowers with purplish red edges.

H. x *hybridus* blooms in a wide range of colors, grows 18" tall and wide and may be deciduous or evergreen. Many cultivars are available.

H. orientalis (lenten rose) is a clump-forming evergreen perennial **Plant of Merit,** 12–24" tall and wide. The white or greenish flowers turn pink as they mature.

Among the earliest harbingers of spring, these beautiful plants should be planted where they can be easily seen.

All parts of hellebores are poisonous and may cause intense discomfort if ingested. The sap may irritate skin on contact.

Features: late-winter to mid-spring flowers in shades of white, green and pink
Height: 12–30" **Spread:** 12–30"
Hardiness: zones 4–9

Hosta

Hosta

These shade-loving plants are pretty tough. They offer such a variety of foliage colors and forms, as well as attractive and often fragrant flowers, that they are indispensable in any shady garden.

Growing

Hostas prefer **light or partial shade** but will grow in full shade; morning sun is preferable to afternoon sun. The ideal soil is **fertile, moist** and **well drained,** but most soils are tolerated. Hostas are fairly drought tolerant, especially if mulched to help retain moisture. Division is not required but can be done every few years in spring or summer to propagate new plants.

Tips

Hostas make wonderful woodland plants and look very attractive when combined with ferns and other fine-textured plants. Hostas work well in mixed borders, particularly when used to hide the leggy lower stems and branches of some shrubs. Their dense growth and thick, shade-providing leaves help suppress weeds.

Recommended

Hundreds of excellent hosta species, cultivars and hybrids do well in Missouri.

H. **Tardiana Group** (*H.* x *tardiana*) is a group of variable hybrids. The cultivars below are **Plant of Merit** selections. '**Halcyon**' is a slug-resistant selection with heart-shaped, blue leaves. It grows 14–16" tall and 28" wide, with lavender

H. sieboldiana 'Elegans' (above)

gray flowers in dense clusters. **'June'** grows 8–12" tall and 24–30" wide. The foliage is greenish gold with blue margins, and the flowers are pale lavender.

H. **'Ginkgo Craig'** has lance-shaped, dark green foliage with narrow white margins. It grows 8–12" tall and 18" wide and bears dark purple flowers.

Also called: plantain lily **Features:** decorative foliage; white or purple flowers in summer and fall **Height:** 7–36" **Spread:** 18"–4' **Hardiness:** zones 3–8

Iris

Iris

I. sibirica (above)
I. germanica 'Stepping Out' (below)

Irises come in many shapes, sizes and colors, and the sharp, vertical lines of iris foliage are an essential component of garden design.

Growing

Irises prefer **full sun** but tolerate very light or dappled shade. The soil should be of **average fertility** and **well drained**. Japanese and Siberian irises prefer a **moist** but still well-drained soil. Deadhead irises to keep them tidy. Cut back the foliage of Siberian irises in spring.

Divide in late summer or early fall. Replant bearded iris rhizomes with the flat side of the foliage fan facing the garden. To help prevent soft rot, allow them to air dry before replanting.

Tips

All irises are popular border plants. Japanese and Siberian irises grow well alongside streams or ponds. Dwarf cultivars look attractive in rock gardens.

Irises can cause severe internal irritation if ingested. Always wash your hands after handling them. Avoid planting irises where children play.

Recommended

Many species and hybrids are available. Among the most popular is bearded iris, often a hybrid of **I. germanica**. It has the widest range of flower colors but is susceptible to iris borer. Several irises are not susceptible, including Japanese iris (**I. ensata**) and Siberian iris (**I. sibirica**).

Features: spring, summer and sometimes fall flowers in many shades of pink, red, purple, blue, white, brown or yellow; attractive foliage
Height: 6"–4' **Spread:** 6"–4'
Hardiness: zones 3–10

Japanese Anemone

Anemone

A. x hybrida (above & below)

Often considered one of the most beautiful flowers, anemone is also one of the last plants to finish flowering in late fall. It does best in an eastern exposure where it is shaded from late afternoon sun.

Growing

Japanese anemone prefers **partial or light shade** but tolerates full sun with adequate moisture and cooler night temperatures. The soil should be of **average to high fertility, humus rich** and **moist**. While dormant, anemone should have dry soil. Mulch Japanese anemone the first winter to help it become established. Divide in spring or fall.

Tips

Japanese anemone makes a beautiful addition to lightly shaded borders, woodland gardens and rock gardens. It looks magnificent when planted en masse. Plant Japanese anemone behind shrubby plants to support the tall stems.

Recommended

A. x *hybrida* is an upright, suckering hybrid that bears pink or white flowers from late summer to early fall. Many cultivars are available. **'Honorine Jobert'** is quite tall and has plentiful white flowers with yellow stamens. It is a **Plant of Merit**. **'Pamina'** has double, pinkish red flowers. **'Whirlwind'** has semi-double, white flowers.

Deadhead Japanese anemone only to keep a tidy look, because removing spent flowers does not extend the blooming period.

Also called: windflower **Features:** pink, red or white flowers; attractive foliage **Height:** 2–5' **Spread:** 24" **Hardiness:** zones 3–8

Lamb's Ears

Stachys

S. byzantina 'Big Ears' (above), *S. byzantina* (below)

It is hard to resist the soft, fuzzy leaves of lamb's ears. They beckon to be touched.

Growing

Lamb's ears grows best in **full sun**. The soil should be of **poor to average fertility** and **well drained**. The leaves can rot in humid weather if the soil is poorly drained.

Remove spent flower spikes to keep the plants looking neat. Cut back diseased or damaged foliage; new foliage will sprout when the weather cools.

Lamb's ears can ramble, but its root system is very shallow. The plants are easily removed from places they aren't wanted.

Tips

Lamb's ears makes a great groundcover in a new garden where the soil has not yet been amended. It can be used to edge borders and pathways, providing a soft, silvery backdrop for more vibrant colors in the border. For a silvery accent, plant a small group of lamb's ears in a border.

Recommended

S. byzantina (*S. lanata*) forms a mat of thick, woolly rosettes of leaves. It bears pinkish purple flowers in summer, but the following cultivars rarely produce flowers. **'Big Ears'** ('Helene von Stein') is an **Emeritus Plant of Merit** that has greenish silver leaves that are twice as big as those of the species. **'Silver Carpet'** has fuzzy, silvery white leaves.

Also called: woolly betony **Features:** pink or purple summer flowers, decorative foliage **Height:** 6–18" **Spread:** 18–24"
Hardiness: zones 3–8

Meadow Rue
Thalictrum

Meadow rues are tall, graceful shade-garden plants with airy flowers that sway gently in summer breezes.

Growing

Meadow rues prefer **light** or **partial shade** but tolerate full sun as long as the soil remains moist. The soil should be **humus rich, moist** and **well drained**. Meadow rues dislike being disturbed, and the plants may take a while to re-establish once they have been divided.

Tips

Meadow rues look beautiful when naturalized in an open woodland or meadow garden. When located in the middle or at the back of a border, they make a soft backdrop for bolder plants and flowers.

Meadow rues often do not emerge until quite late in spring. Place a marker where you have planted them so that you do not inadvertently disturb the roots when cultivating.

Recommended

*T. **aquilegifolium*** (columbine meadow rue) forms an upright mound with pink or white plumes of flowers. Cultivars are available.

*T. **rochebruneanum*** 'Lavender Mist' (lavender mist meadow rue) forms a narrow, upright clump. This **Plant of Merit** bears blooms of lavender purple with numerous distinctive yellow stamens.

T. aquilegifolium (above & below)

Tall meadow rues may need some support if they are in an exposed location where a strong wind may topple them.

Features: pink, purple, yellow or white summer flowers; light, airy habit; attractive foliage
Height: 2–5' **Spread:** 12–36"
Hardiness: zones 3–8

Peony

Paeonia

P. lactiflora 'Shimmering Velvet' (above)
P. lactiflora cultivars (below)

Peonies are among the longest-lived perennials. They are easy to grow and tough as nails, and they add backbone to the garden in a way few other perennials can match.

Growing

Peonies prefer **full sun** but tolerate some shade. Peonies like **fertile, humus-rich, moist, well-drained** soil with a lot of **compost**. Prepare the soil before introducing the plants. Mulch peonies lightly with compost in spring. Too much fertilizer, particularly nitrogen, causes floppy growth and retards blooming.

Divide in fall to propagate plants. Deadhead to keep the plants looking tidy. Clean up around peonies in fall to reduce the possibility of disease.

Tips

Peonies look great in a border combined with other early bloomers. Avoid planting peonies under trees, where they have to compete for moisture and nutrients.

Tubers planted too shallowly or, more commonly, too deeply will not flower. The buds or eyes on the tuber should be 1–2" below the soil surface.

Place wire tomato or peony cages around the plants in early spring to support the heavy flowers. The growing foliage will hide the cage.

Recommended

Hundreds of peony species and cultivars offer possibly fragrant, single or double flowers in a wide range of colors. Visit your local garden center to see what is available.

Features: white, cream white, yellow, pink, red or purple flowers in spring and early summer; attractive foliage **Height:** 24–36" **Spread:** 24–36" **Hardiness:** zones 2–7

Perennial Salvia

Salvia

Perennial salvias are reliable, hardy members of the perennial border.

Growing

Perennial salvias prefer **full sun** and tolerate light shade. The soil should be of **average fertility, humus rich** and **well drained**. Established plants tolerate drought.

Deadhead to prolong blooming. Trim the plants back in spring to encourage new growth and keep them tidy; new shoots will sprout from old, woody growth.

Tips

Perennial salvias are attractive plants for the middle or front of the border. They can also be grown in mixed planters.

Recommended

S. azurea var. *grandiflora* (azure sage) is an open, upright plant that produces azure blue blooms in late summer and into fall. (Zones 5–9)

S. nemorosa (*S. x superba*) is a clump-forming, branching plant with gray-green leaves and spikes of blue or purple summer flowers. (Zones 3–7)

S. x sylvestris (violet sage) has grayish green foliage and long-lasting, deep violet blue flower spikes. **'May Night'** bears large, deep blue flowers. (Zones 5–9)

S. verticillata **'Purple Rain'** is a low, mounding plant with crinkled foliage. It bears light red to violet blooms all summer. (Zones 5–8)

S. nemorosa 'East Friesland' (above)
S. azurea (below)

Perennial salvias can be divided in spring, but they are slow to re-establish and resent having their roots disturbed.

Also called: sage **Features:** attractive purple, violet, blue or light red flowers; foliage
Height: 1–4' **Spread:** 18–36"
Hardiness: zones 3–9

Pincushion Flower

Scabiosa

S. 'Butterfly Blue' (above)

If you are creating an old-fashioned, informal style of garden, be sure to include pincushion flower's mounds of dark green foliage and profusion of lacy, lavender blue blooms.

Growing

Pincushion flower prefers **full sun** but tolerates partial shade. The soil should be **light, moderately fertile, neutral or alkaline** and **well drained**. Divide in early spring, whenever the clumps become overgrown.

Deadhead to promote a longer flowering period. Leave the evergreen foliage intact over winter and remove dead and tattered leaves in spring.

Tips

Pincushion flowers look best planted in groups of three or more in a bed or border. They are also used as cut flowers.

Recommended

Several hybrids have been developed from crosses between *S. caucasica* and *S. columbaria*. These hybrids may be listed as cultivars of either species. **'Butterfly Blue'** is a **Plant of Merit** that grows 12–24" tall and bears lavender blue flowers from early summer until fall frost. **'Pink Mist'** grows about 18" tall and bears many lavender pink blooms from summer to fall frost.

Pincushion flower survives Missouri winters, but summer heat and humidity often sap the plant of strength, making it short-lived in the southern part of the state.

Features: purple, blue, white or pink flowers from summer to fall; attractive foliage
Height: 12–24" **Spread:** 24"
Hardiness: zones 3–7

Purple Coneflower

Echinacea

Purple coneflower is an attractive, easy-to-grow, long-lived prairie native that grows well in Missouri gardens.

Growing

Purple coneflower grows well in **full sun** or very **light shade**. It prefers an **average to rich** soil, but it tolerates any soil as long as it is **well drained**. The thick taproots make this plant drought resistant, but it prefers to have regular water. Divide in spring or fall every four years or so.

Deadhead early in the season to prolong flowering. Later you may wish to leave the flowerheads in place to self-seed and provide winter interest. Pinch the plants back or thin out the stems in early summer to encourage bushy growth that is less prone to mildew.

Tips

Use purple coneflowers in meadow gardens and informal borders, either in groups or as single specimens. The dry flowerheads make an interesting feature in fall and winter gardens.

Recommended

E. purpurea is an upright plant covered in prickly hairs. It bears purple flowers with orangy centers. Cultivars are available that bloom in white and shades of purple. White-flowered plants tend to be shorter and not as long-lived as the purple-flowered plants.

Also called: coneflower, echinacea
Features: purple, pink or white flowers with rusty orange centers from mid-summer to fall; persistent seedheads **Height:** 18"–4'
Spread: 12–24" **Hardiness:** zones 3–8

E. purpurea (above & below)

Purple coneflower attracts butterflies and other wildlife to the garden, providing pollen, nectar and seeds to the various hungry visitors.

Rosinweed

Silphium

S. perfoliatum (above & below)

Rosinweeds are big, bold Missouri natives that can reach heights of eight to ten feet.

Growing

Rosinweeds grow well in **full sun** or **partial shade,** but they flop with too much shade. The soil should be of **average fertility, neutral to alkaline** and **moist.** They tolerate heavy clay soils. The plants can be divided in spring, but the large root mass may require the efforts of two people to divide it. The roots of some species can reach 10–15' deep.

Tips

These tall plants can be used in prairie and meadow plantings, at the back of borders, along the edges of woodland gardens, in bog gardens and in waterside plantings.

Recommended

S. laciniatum (compass plant) forms an upright clump of hairy stems. This **Plant of Merit** bears clusters of daisy-like, yellow flowers in late summer and fall.

S. perfoliatum (cup plant) forms an upright clump of hairless stems. It bears clusters of daisy-like, yellow flowers with darker centers from mid-summer to fall.

The leaves of compass plant always orient themselves to face east and west, and the flowers always face east. Be sure to locate compass plant on the west side of the garden so you can best admire it.

Features: yellow summer and fall flowers; adaptable; plant size **Height:** 8–10' **Spread:** 3–5' **Hardiness:** zones 5–9

Russian Sage

Perovskia

P. atriplicifolia (above), *P. atriplicifolia* 'Filigran' (below)

Russian sage is an easy-to-grow, long-lived perennial that features a lengthy blooming period through late summer.

Growing

Russian sage prefers **full sun**. The soil should be **poor to moderately fertile** and **well drained**. Too much water and nitrogen cause this plant to flop, so do not plant it next to heavy feeders. Russian sage cannot be divided.

To encourage vigorous, bushy growth, cut the plant back hard to about 6–12" in spring, when new growth appears low on the branches, or in fall.

Tips

The silvery foliage and blue flowers work well with other plants in the back of a mixed border and soften the appearance of daylilies. Russian sage can also create a soft screen in a natural garden or on a dry bank.

Recommended

P. atriplicifolia is a loose, upright plant with finely divided, silvery white foliage. This **Emeritus Plant of Merit** has small, lavender blue flowers that are loosely held on branched, silvery stems. **'Filigran'** has delicate foliage and an upright habit.

To assist Russian sage in surviving winter, plant the crowns high in the soil or in a raised bed to keep winter moisture from collecting. Light mulch and a sheltered location also help.

Features: blue or purple mid-summer to fall flowers; attractive habit; fragrant, gray-green foliage **Height:** 3–4' **Spread:** 3–4' **Hardiness:** zones 4–9

Sedum
Sedum

S. *acre* (above), S. 'Autumn Joy' (below)

Some 300 to 500 species of sedums are distributed throughout the Northern Hemisphere. Many are grown for their foliage, which ranges in color from steel gray-blue and green to red and burgundy.

'Autumn Joy' sedums bring color to the late-season garden, when few flowers are in bloom.

Growing

Sedums prefer **full sun** but tolerate partial shade. The soil should be of **average fertility, very well drained** and **neutral to alkaline.** Divide in spring when needed.

Tips

Low-growing sedums make wonderful groundcovers and additions to rock gardens or rock walls. They edge beds and borders beautifully. Tall sedums give a lovely late-season display in a bed or border.

Recommended

S. acre (gold moss stonecrop) is a low-growing, wide-spreading plant with small, yellow-green flowers.

S. **'Autumn Joy'** (autumn joy sedum) is an upright hybrid. The flowers open pink or red and fade to deep bronze.

S. kamtschaticum produces a low-growing carpet of scalloped, green foliage covered with starry, bright yellow flowers.

S. spectabile (showy stonecrop) is an upright species with pink flowers. Cultivars are available.

S. spurium (two-row stonecrop) forms a low, wide mat of foliage with deep pink or white flowers.

Also called: stonecrop **Features:** yellow, white, red or pink flowers from summer to fall; decorative fleshy foliage; easy to grow
Height: 2–24" **Spread:** 12" to indefinite
Hardiness: zones 3–8

Spike Speedwell

Veronica

V. spicata 'Sunny Border Blue' (above), *V. spicata* 'Red Fox' (below)

Spike speedwells are excellent, long-lived perennials for new gardeners to start with.

Growing

Spike speedwells prefer **full sun** but tolerate partial shade. The soil should be of **average fertility, moist** and **well drained**. Lack of sun and excessive moisture and nitrogen may be partly to blame for the sloppy habits of some speedwells. Divide in fall or spring every two or three years to ensure strong, vigorous growth and decrease the chances of flopping.

To encourage rapid reblooming when the flowers begin to fade, remove the entire spike where it joins the plant. For tidy plants, shear back to 6" in June.

Tips

Low-growing spike speedwells are useful in a rock garden or at the front of a perennial border. Upright spike speedwells work well in masses in a bed or border.

Recommended

V. **'Goodness Grows'** is a popular, easy, long-blooming plant that grows to about 12" tall and wide and produces long, tapering spikes of small, blue-violet flowers.

V. spicata (spike speedwell) is a low, mounding plant with stems that flop over when they get too tall. It grows 12–24" tall, spreads 18" and bears spikes of blue flowers. **'Red Fox'** has dark red-pink flowers. **'Sunny Border Blue'** has bright blue flowers.

Features: white, pink, purple or blue summer flowers; varied habits **Height:** 12–24" **Spread:** 12–18" **Hardiness:** zones 3–8

Toad Lily

Tricyrtis

T. hirta cultivar (above), T. hirta (below)

Toad lily foliage may suffer tip burn if the plant is under stress or if it gets too hot, but it won't harm the plant.

You have to get up close to appreciate toad lily's small, unusual flowers.

Growing

Toad lily grows well in **partial shade, light shade** or **full shade**. The soil should be **fertile, humus rich, moist** and **well drained**.

Tips

This diminutive plant is well suited to woodland gardens and shaded borders. If you have a shaded rock garden, patio or pond, toad lily makes a good addition to locations where you can approach for a good look at the peculiar spotted, almost orchid-like flowers.

Recommended

T. formosana (*T. stolonifera*) is an erect, low-maintenance perennial that spreads slowly by stolons. A **Plant of Merit,** it has shiny, dark green foliage and white to pale lavender flowers that are heavily purple-spotted.

T. hirta (Japanese toad lily) forms a clump of arching stems that bear light green leaves. It produces white flowers with purple to maroon spots in late summer and fall. Many wonderful cultivars are available.

Features: late-summer and fall flowers in white, blue, purple or maroon, with or without spots; attractive foliage **Height:** 24–36" **Spread:** 12–24" **Hardiness:** zones 4–9

Arborvitae

Thuja

T. occidentalis 'Sherwood Moss' (above), *T. occidentalis* (below)

Arborvitae makes a gorgeous backdrop for perennial and shrub borders. Rot resistant, durable, adaptable and long-lived, arborvitae is a great plant for Missouri gardens.

Growing

Arborvitae prefers **full sun**. The soil should be of **average fertility, moist** and **well drained**. Arborvitae enjoys humidity and is often found growing near marshy areas. Arborvitae performs best with some shelter from wind, especially in winter, when the foliage can easily dry out and give the entire plant a rather drab, brown appearance.

Tips

Large varieties of arborvitae make excellent specimen trees, and smaller cultivars can be used in foundation plantings or shrub borders or as formal or informal hedges.

Recommended

T. occidentalis (eastern arborvitae, eastern white cedar) is a narrow, pyramidal tree with scale-like needles. Many diverse cultivars are available, including pyramidal forms that make excellent specimens, yellow types that add color to the winter landscape and dwarf, globe-shaped forms for the mixed border or rock garden. The cultivars may be less cold hardy than the species.

Deer enjoy eating the foliage of T. occidentalis. *However, western arborvitae* (T. plicata) *is relatively deer resistant.*

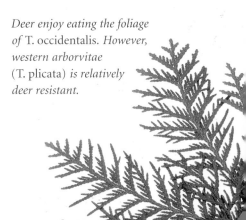

Features: foliage; bark; form **Habit:** small to large, evergreen shrub or tree **Height:** 18"–50'
Spread: 18"–15' **Hardiness:** zones 2–7

Bald-Cypress
Taxodium

T. distichum (above & below)

Bald-cypress is a tough, dependable tree that grows well in a variety of conditions and climates.

Growing

Bald-cypress prefers **full sun** and **acidic, moist** soil, but it can adapt to most soils and conditions. Highly alkaline soil may cause the foliage to turn yellow (chlorotic). Bald-cypress develops a deep taproot but transplants fairly easily when young.

Tips

Bald-cypress can be used as a specimen tree or in a group planting. This fairly large tree looks best with plenty of space. It is ideal in a swampy or frequently wet area where few other trees would thrive.

When grown in waterlogged soil or near a water feature, bald-cypress develops gnome-like "knees," which are knobby roots that poke up from the water.

Recommended

T. distichum is a slender, conical tree that may grow over 100' tall in the wild. With maturity, it becomes irregular and more rounded, and the trunk becomes buttressed. In fall, the blue-green foliage turns a rusty orange before falling.

To the uninformed, bald-cypress appears to be an evergreen. Gasps are often heard when this deciduous conifer turns color in fall and defoliates. Plant it near water to double the effect of its fall color.

Features: attractive summer and fall foliage; attractive habit; cones; attractive trunk
Habit: conical, deciduous, coniferous tree
Height: 50–70' **Spread:** 18–30'
Hardiness: zones 4–9

Barberry
Berberis

Barberries are dependable, easy-to-grow shrubs with many variations in plant size, foliage color and fruit. The plants have extremely sharp spines, so place them where they can be visually stimulating but away from paths and walkways.

Growing

Barberry develops the best fall color when grown in **full sun,** but it tolerates partial shade. Any **well-drained** soil is suitable. This plant tolerates drought and urban conditions but suffers in poorly drained, wet soil.

Tips

Barberries can be included in shrub and mixed beds and borders. Large barberries make great hedges that are very effective for discouraging foot (or dog) traffic from cutting through your yard. Small cultivars can be grown in rock gardens, in raised beds or along rock walls.

Recommended

B. thunbergii (Japanese barberry) is a dense shrub with a broad, rounded habit. The foliage is bright green and turns variable shades of orange, red or purple in fall. Yellow spring flowers are followed by glossy, red fruit later in summer. Many cultivars have been developed for their variable foliage color, including shades of purple, yellow or variegated varieties. **'Rose Glow'** has purple foliage variegated with white and pink splotches. It grows 5–6' tall and wide or slightly wider.

B. thunbergii 'Rose Glow' (above)
B. thunbergii 'Atropurpurea' (below)

B. thunbergii is being noted as an invasive species in shaded, well-drained natural habitats. Its seeds are typically distributed by birds. The cultivars are less invasive.

Features: foliage; flowers; fruit
Habit: prickly, deciduous shrub **Height:** 2–6'
Spread: 18"–6' **Hardiness:** zones 4–8

Beech
Fagus

F. *grandiflora* (above), F. *sylvatica* (below)

The majestic beeches are certainly not the fastest growing trees, but they are among the most beautiful. They are great as large shade trees.

Beechnuts are edible when roasted.

Growing

Beeches grow equally well in **full sun** or **partial shade**. The soil should be of **average fertility, loamy** and **well drained,** although almost all well-drained soils are tolerated. American beech suffers in alkaline and poorly drained soils.

American beech doesn't like having its roots disturbed and should be transplanted only when very young. European beech transplants easily and is more tolerant of varied soil conditions than is American beech.

Tips

Beeches make excellent specimens. They are also used as shade trees and in woodland gardens. These trees need a lot of space, but the European beech's adaptability to pruning makes it a reasonable choice in a small garden.

Recommended

F. grandifolia (American beech) is a broad-canopied tree native to most of eastern North America.

F. sylvatica (European beech) is a spectacular broad tree with a number of interesting cultivars. Several are small enough to use in the home garden. The range includes narrow, columnar and weeping varieties to selections with purple or yellow leaves or variegated foliage of pink, white and green.

Features: foliage; bark; habit; fall color; fruit
Habit: large, oval, deciduous shade tree
Height: 30–80' **Spread:** 10–65'
Hardiness: zones 4–9

Black Gum

Nyssa

Black gum is a slow-growing, native beauty with wonderful glossy, bright green foliage that turns vivid shades of yellow, orange, scarlet and purple in fall.

Growing

Black gum grows well in **full sun** or **partial shade**. The soil should be **average to fertile, neutral to acidic** and **well drained**. Provide a location with shelter from strong winds. Plant this tree when young and don't attempt to move it again. Black gum can take a while to get established and dislikes having its roots disturbed.

Tips

Black gum is a beautiful specimen tree. It can be used as a street tree, but not in polluted situations. Planted singly or in groups, it is attractive and small enough for a medium-sized property.

Recommended

N. sylvatica (sour gum, black tupelo) is a Missouri native and a **Plant of Merit**. This small to medium-sized, pyramidal to rounded tree can grow in very wet or somewhat dry conditions. It generally grows 30–50' tall but can reach 100' over time. It spreads about 20–30'. The mature bark resembles alligator hide. Cultivars offer special characteristics, such as weeping branches or a narrow, upright growth habit.

Black gum fruit attracts birds but is too sour for human tastes.

N. sylvatica (above), *N. sylvatica* cultivar (below)

Features: attractive habit; decorative summer and fall foliage; bark **Habit:** pyramidal to rounded, deciduous tree **Height:** 10–50'; occasionally more **Spread:** 6–30' **Hardiness:** zones 4–9

Bluebeard

Caryopteris

C. x *clandonensis* cultivar (above)
C. x *clandonensis* (below)

Bluebeard is a cheerful, easy-to-grow shrub. The flowers and foliage provide outstanding contrast to purple-leaved plants.

Bluebeard is cultivated for its aromatic stems, foliage and flowers.

Growing

Bluebeard prefers **full sun** but tolerates light shade. It does best in soil of **average fertility** that is **light** and **well drained**. Wet and poorly drained soils can kill this plant. Bluebeard is very drought tolerant once it is established.

Cut the plant back to within 2–6" of the ground in early spring; flowers will form on the new growth that emerges. Deadheading or lightly shearing once the flowers begin to fade may encourage more flowering.

Tips

Include bluebeard in your shrub or mixed border. The bright blue of the late-season flowers is welcome when many other plants are past their flowering best. This plant can be treated as a herbaceous perennial in areas where it is killed back each winter.

Recommended

C. x *clandonensis* forms a dense mound and bears clusters of blue or purple flowers in late summer and early fall. **'Longwood Blue'** is a large, mound-forming **Emeritus Plant of Merit** that grows 4' tall and wide. It has light violet-blue flowers and gray-green foliage. **'Worcester Gold'** has bright yellow-green foliage that contrasts vividly with the violet-blue flowers of late summer.

Also called: bluebird, blue spirea
Features: flowers; foliage; fragrance; easy to grow **Habit:** rounded, spreading, deciduous shrub **Height:** 2–4' **Spread:** 2–6'
Hardiness: zones 5–8

Boxwood

Buxus

B. microphylla var. *koreana* x *B. sempervirens* cultivars (above & below)

Boxwoods are versatile evergreens. They can be pruned to form neat hedges, geometric shapes or fanciful creatures. When allowed to grow naturally, boxwoods form attractive rounded mounds.

Growing

Boxwoods prefer **partial shade** but adapt to full shade or to full sun if kept well watered. The soil should be **fertile** and **well drained**. Established boxwoods tolerate drought.

Using mulch benefits these shallow-rooted shrubs. It is best not to disturb the earth around established boxwoods.

Tips

These shrubs make excellent background plants in mixed borders. They are also immune to deer browsing—a key feature in many neighborhoods.

Recommended

Several cultivars developed from crossing *B. microphylla* var. *koreana* and *B. sempervirens* exhibit good hardiness and pest resistance, and they have attractive year-round foliage. **'Green Velvet'** is a compact selection reaching 36" in height.

B. sinica insularis **'Wintergreen'** is a dense, mounding shrub, slowly growing to 2–4' tall and 3–5' wide. The foliage keeps its light green color through winter.

Boxwood foliage contains toxic compounds; when ingested, it can cause severe digestive upset and possibly death.

Features: foliage; slow, even growth
Habit: dense, rounded, evergreen shrub
Height: 2–8' **Spread:** equal to or slightly greater than height **Hardiness:** zones 4–8

Carolina Allspice

Calycanthus

C. floridus (above & below)

Growing

Carolina allspice grows well in **full sun to full shade,** in **moist, fertile** soil **rich in organic matter**. Ensure you provide regular water. Prune only to remove dead, diseased or damaged branches.

Carolina allspice is very easy to grow from seed or by layering branches.

Tips

Carolina allspice is effective as a background shrub in a mixed or shrub bed or as screening. If left unattended, it forms a thicket. Excess suckers can be dug up and transplanted or tossed away.

Recommended

C. floridus is a vigorous, deciduous shrub that spreads by suckers. In late spring and early summer it produces brown-tipped, deep red flowers that resemble small water lilies and have a sweet aroma. The lush, dark green leaves have a camphor-like odor when bruised or crushed; they turn yellow in fall. The wood and bark are also aromatic. The seeds of this **Plant of Merit** are poisonous and should not be eaten. **'Athens'** has very fragrant, yellow flowers.

Plant Carolina allspice near pathways or entryways so that passersby can appreciate the fragrance of the blooms.

With Carolina allspice, the amount of fragrance varies from plant to plant. Purchasing it in bloom ensures you get an aromatic plant.

Also called: spicebush, sweet shrub, pineapple shrub, strawberry bush **Features:** red or yellow flowers; fragrance; handsome foliage; easy to grow **Habit:** rounded to irregular, multi-stemmed shrub **Height:** 5–8' **Spread:** 5–8' **Hardiness:** zones 5–9

Crabapple
Malus

The beautiful display of spring flowers, autumn color and winter fruit makes crabapples enjoyable all year long.

Growing
Crabapples prefer **full sun** but tolerate partial shade. The soil should be of **average to rich fertility, moist** and **well drained**. These trees tolerate damp soil.

One of the best ways to prevent the spread of crabapple pests and diseases is to clean up all the leaves and fruit that fall off the tree. Many pests overwinter in the fruit, leaves or soil at the base of the tree. Clearing away their winter shelter helps keep populations under control.

Tips
Crabapples make excellent specimen plants. Many varieties are quite small, so there is one to suit almost any size of garden. Some are even small enough to grow in large containers. Crabapples are good choices for creating espalier specimens along a wall or fence.

Recommended
Hundreds of crabapple selections are available. When choosing a species, variety or cultivar, look for disease resistance. **'Mary Potter'** is a densely branched, disease-resistant, rounded tree that grows 10–15' tall and 15–20' wide. This **Plant of Merit** has bright pink buds that open to white flowers, covering the tree in spring. It has dark green foliage and shiny, bright red fruit.

Be sure to properly prune crabapples while they are young to help them become the unique mature specimens that are so universally admired.

Features: spring flowers; late-season and winter fruit; decorative fall foliage; habit; bark **Habit:** rounded, mounded or spreading, small to medium, deciduous tree **Height:** 5–30' **Spread:** 6–30' **Hardiness:** zones 4–8

Dogwood
Cornus

C. florida (above), *C. kousa* var. *chinensis* (below)

Whether your garden is wet, dry, sunny or shaded, there is a dogwood for almost every condition.

Growing

Tree dogwoods grow well in **light shade** or **partial shade**. Shrub dogwoods prefer **full sun** or **partial shade**, with the best stem colors developing in full sun. The soil should be of **average to high fertility, high in organic matter, neutral to slightly**

C. florida is the state tree of Missouri.

acidic and **well drained**. Shrub dogwoods prefer moist soil. *C. sericea* tolerates wet soil.

Tips

Use shrub dogwoods in a shrub or mixed border. They look best planted in groups. The tree species make wonderful specimen plants and are small enough to include in most gardens.

Recommended

C. florida (flowering dogwood, American dogwood) is a small tree with horizontally layered branches and showy pink or white blossoms. (Zones 5–9)

C. kousa var. *chinensis* (Chinese dogwood) is a **Plant of Merit**. This small tree has interesting bark, early-summer flowers, bright red fruit and red to purple fall foliage. (Zones 5–9)

C. mas **'Golden Glory'** is a large shrub that bears a plethora of yellow flower clusters in late winter. Tart, edible, bright red fruit appears in late summer. The foliage turns shades of red and purple in fall. It is a **Plant of Merit**. (Zones 4–9)

C. sericea (*C. stolonifera;* red-osier dogwood, red-twig dogwood) has bright red stems, small, white flowers and red to orange fall color. **'Cardinal'** is a **Plant of Merit** with pinkish red stems that become bright red in winter. (Zones 2–8)

Features: late-spring to early-summer flowers; colorful fall foliage; stem color; fruit; habit
Habit: deciduous shrub or small tree
Height: 5–30' **Spread:** 5–30'
Hardiness: zones 2–9

False Cypress
Chamaecyparis

False cypresses come in a wide variety of colors, sizes, shapes and growth habits not available in most other evergreens.

Growing

False cypresses prefer **full sun**. The soil should be **fertile, moist, neutral to acidic** and **well drained**. Alkaline soils are tolerated. In shaded areas, growth may be sparse or thin. In northern Missouri, the climate extremes can be hard on false cypresses.

Tips

Tree varieties are used as specimen plants and for hedging. The dwarf and slow-growing cultivars are used in borders and rock gardens and as bonsai. False cypress shrubs can be grown near the house or as evergreen specimens in large containers.

Recommended

Several species and many cultivars of false cypress are available. The scaly foliage can be in a drooping or strand form, in fan-like or feathery sprays, and they may be dark green, bright green or yellow. Plant forms vary too, from mounding or rounded to tall and pyramidal or narrow with pendulous branches.

C. pisifera '**Filifera Aurea**' (golden threadleaf false cypress) is a slow-growing **Plant of Merit** selection that has thread-like, golden yellow foliage. It grows about 40' tall and 10–20' wide.

C. pisifera 'Filifera Aurea' (above & below)

The oils in the foliage of false cypresses may irritate sensitive skin.

Features: foliage; habit; cones **Habit:** narrow, pyramidal, evergreen tree or shrub
Height: 10"–100' **Spread:** 1–55'
Hardiness: zones 4–8

Fothergilla
Fothergilla

F. gardenii 'Blue Mist' (above), *F. major* (below)

Foliage is a key element in a well-planned garden. Fothergillas have lovely gray-green leaves that stand out against evergreens in a woodland garden. They also boast fiery fall foliage.

Growing

Fothergillas produce the most flowers and the best fall color in **full sun,** but they also grow well in **partial shade.** The soil should be of **average fertility, acidic, humus rich, moist** and **well drained.**

Fothergilla flowers have no petals. The showy parts are the white stamens.

Tips

Fothergillas are attractive and useful in shrub or mixed borders, in woodland gardens and when combined with evergreen groundcover.

Recommended

Cultivars are available for both species below.

F. gardenii (dwarf fothergilla) is a bushy shrub, 24–36" tall and wide, that bears fragrant white flowers before the foliage emerges. The foliage turns yellow, orange and red in fall. It is a **Plant of Merit.**

F. major (large fothergilla) is a large, rounded shrub that bears fragrant, white flowers just before or with the emerging foliage. The fall colors are yellow, orange and scarlet.

Also called: bottlebrush **Features:** spring flowers; scent; attractive fall foliage
Habit: dense, rounded or bushy, deciduous shrub
Height: 2–10' **Spread:** 2–10'
Hardiness: zones 4–8

Fringe Tree
Chionanthus

Fringe trees are cold hardy and adapt to a wide range of growing conditions. They bear lacy, sweetly scented, white flowers over a long period in early summer.

Growing

Fringe trees prefer **full sun** but also grow in partial shade. They do best in soil that is **fertile, moist** and **well drained** but adapt to most soil conditions. In the wild, they are often found growing alongside stream banks.

Tips

Fringe trees work well as specimen plants, as part of a border or beside a water feature. They begin flowering at a very early age. Both male and female plants must be present for the females to set fruit. Some trees have both male and female flowers.

C. virginicus (above & below)

Recommended

C. virginicus (white fringe tree) is a spreading small tree or large shrub that bears drooping, fragrant, white flowers. It is a Missouri native and a **Plant of Merit**.

These small, pollution-tolerant trees are good choices for city gardens, and the dark purplish fruit attracts birds.

Features: early-summer flowers; fall and winter fruit; bark; habit **Habit:** rounded or spreading, deciduous, large shrub or small tree
Height: 10–25' **Spread:** 10–25'
Hardiness: zones 4–9

Golden Rain Tree
Koelreuteria

K. paniculata (above & below)

With its delicate clusters of yellow flowers and overall lacy appearance in summer, this lovely tree deserves wider use as a specimen or shade tree.

Growing
Golden rain tree grows best in **full sun**. The soil should be **average to fertile, moist** and **well drained**. This tree tolerates heat, drought, wind and air pollution. It also adapts to most pH levels and different soil types.

Golden rain tree is one of the few trees with yellow flowers and one of the few trees to flower in mid- or late summer.

Tips
Golden rain tree makes an excellent shade or specimen tree for small properties. Its ability to adapt to a wide range of soils makes it useful in many garden situations. The fruit is not messy and will not stain adjacent patios or decks.

Recommended
K. paniculata is an attractive, rounded, spreading tree that grows 30–40' tall and wide. It bears long clusters of small, yellow flowers in mid-summer, followed by capsular, red-tinged, green fruit. The leaves are attractive and somewhat lacy in appearance. The foliage may turn bright yellow in fall.

Features: attractive foliage; unique fruit; yellow mid- or late-summer flowers
Habit: fast-growing, rounded, spreading, deciduous tree **Height:** 25–40'
Spread: 6–40' **Hardiness:** zones 5–8

Holly
Ilex

Hollies vary greatly in shape and size. They require careful attention to their soil conditions.

Growing
These plants prefer **full sun** but tolerate partial shade. The soil should be of **average to rich fertility, acidic, humus rich** and **moist.** Shelter plants from winter wind to help prevent the leaves from drying out. Apply a summer mulch to keep the roots cool and moist.

Tips
Hollies can be used in woodland gardens and in shrub and mixed borders. They can also be shaped into hedges. Inkberry looks much like boxwood and has similar uses in the landscape. Winterberry is good for naturalizing in moist sites.

Recommended
I. glabra (inkberry) is a rounded shrub with evergreen glossy, deep green foliage and dark purple fruit. It grows 6–10' tall and spreads 8–10'. (Zones 4–9)

I. opaca (American holly) is an evergreen tree with minimally toothed, leathery, dark green leaves and red fruit. It can grow 40–50' tall and spread 20–40' but is often smaller in gardens. (Zones 5–9)

I. verticillata (winterberry) **'Nana'** (RED SPRITE) is a deciduous, dwarf cultivar that grows 3–4' tall and wide and bears bright red fruit. It is a **Plant of Merit.**

I. opaca (above)

Hollies have male and female flowers on separate plants, and both must be present for the females to set fruit.

Features: glossy, sometimes spiny foliage; fruit; habit **Habit:** erect or spreading, evergreen or deciduous shrub or tree
Height: 3–50' **Spread:** 3–40'
Hardiness: zones 3–9

Hornbeam

Carpinus

C. caroliniana (above), *C. betulus* 'Fastigiata' (below)

Growing

Hornbeams prefer **full sun** or **partial shade**. The soil should be **average to fertile** and **well drained**. American hornbeam favors moist, acidic soil conditions and grows well near ponds and streams.

Tips

These small- to medium-sized trees can be used as specimens or shade trees in small gardens or can be pruned to form hedges. The narrow, upright cultivars are often used to create barriers and windbreaks.

Recommended

C. betulus (European hornbeam) is a pyramidal to rounded tree. The foliage turns bright yellow or orange in fall. **'Fastigiata'** is a **Plant of Merit**. It is an upright cultivar that is narrow when young but broadens as it matures. It grows 50' tall and spreads 40'. (Zones 4–8)

C. caroliniana (American hornbeam, ironwood, musclewood, bluebeech) is a small, slow-growing Missouri native tree that tolerates shade and city conditions. The foliage of this **Plant of Merit** turns yellow to red or purple in fall.

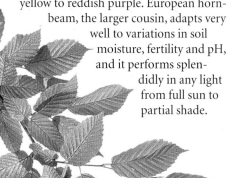

American hornbeam is great for use in city lots or anywhere a handsome, smallish tree is needed in partial shade. The fall color is outstanding, from yellow to reddish purple. European hornbeam, the larger cousin, adapts very well to variations in soil moisture, fertility and pH, and it performs splendidly in any light from full sun to partial shade.

Hornbeam leaves remain a fresh bright green through the oppressive humidity of summer.

Features: habit; fall color **Habit:** pyramidal, deciduous tree **Height:** 10–70'
Spread: 10–50' **Hardiness:** zones 3–9

Horsechestnut · Buckeye

Aesculus

A. parviflora (above), A. x carnea (below)

Horsechestnuts are extremely attractive trees and shrubs that feature attractive foliage and wide-ranging options for size, habit and bloom color.

Growing

Horsechestnuts grow well in **full sun** or **partial shade,** in **fertile, moist, well-drained** soil. These trees dislike drought.

Tips

Horsechestnuts are used as specimen and shade trees. They give heavy shade, which is excellent for cooling buildings but makes it difficult to grow grass beneath them. The roots of horsechestnuts can break up sidewalks and patios if planted too close.

The small, shrubby horsechestnuts grow well near pond plantings and also make interesting specimens. They can also form large colonies.

Recommended

A. x carnea (red horsechestnut) is a dense, rounded to spreading tree that grows 30–50' tall and 25–45' wide. It has dark pink flowers. (Zones 4–8)

A. parviflora (bottlebrush buckeye) is a spreading, mound-forming, suckering shrub that grows 8–12' tall and 8–15' wide. This **Plant of Merit** bears abundant, creamy white flowers.

A. pavia (red buckeye) is a low-growing to rounded, shrubby tree with cherry red flowers and handsome foliage. This Missouri native and **Plant of Merit** selection needs consistent moisture. It grows 12–18' tall and wide. (Zones 4–8)

All parts of Aesculus plants, especially the seeds, are toxic.

Features: early-summer flowers; foliage; spiny fruit **Habit:** rounded or spreading, deciduous tree or shrub **Height:** 8–50' **Spread:** 8–45' **Hardiness:** zones 4–9

Hydrangea

Hydrangea

H. quercifolia (above)
H. macrophylla cultivars (below)

Hydrangeas offer a good selection of worthwhile blooming shrubs with long-lasting flowers and glossy, green leaves, some of which turn beautiful colors in fall.

Growing

Hydrangeas grow well in **full sun** or **partial shade,** and shade or partial shade reduces leaf and flower scorch in hot regions; *H. arborescens* tolerates heavy shade. The soil should be of **average to high fertility, humus rich, moist** and **well drained**.

Tips

Hydrangeas come in many forms and have many uses in the landscape. They can be included in shrub or mixed borders, used as specimens or informal barriers or planted in groups or containers.

Recommended

H. arborescens (smooth hydrangea) is a rounded shrub that flowers well even in shade. Its cultivars bear large clusters of showy, white blossoms. It is a Missouri native and a **Plant of Merit.**

H. macrophylla (bigleaf hydrangea) is a rounded or mounding shrub that bears pink or blue flowers in mid- to late summer.

H. paniculata (panicle hydrangea) is a spreading to upright large shrub or small tree that bears white flowers.

H. quercifolia (oakleaf hydrangea) is a mound-forming **Plant of Merit** with attractive, exfoliating bark and large, oak-like leaves that turn bronze to bright red in fall. Conical clusters of sterile and fertile white flowers appear in mid-summer.

Features: flowers; habit; foliage; bark
Habit: deciduous; mounding or spreading shrub or tree **Height:** 3–25' **Spread:** 3–20'
Hardiness: zones 4–8

Juniper

Juniperus

J. horizontalis 'Blue Chip' (above), *J. horizontalis* 'Blue Prince' (below)

Junipers are extremely durable and adaptable evergreen shrubs that come in a wide variety of forms, colors and textures. There is sure to be one to fit your landscape.

Growing

Junipers prefer **full sun** but tolerate light shade. The soil should be of **average fertility** and **well drained,** but these plants tolerate most conditions.

Tips

Junipers make prickly barriers, hedges or windbreaks. They can be used in borders, as specimens or in groups. The low-growing species can be used in rock gardens and as groundcover. For interesting evergreen color, mix the yellow-foliaged junipers with blue-needled varieties.

Recommended

Junipers vary from species to species and often from cultivar to cultivar within a species. **J. chinensis** (Chinese juniper) is a conical tree or spreading shrub. **J. horizontalis** (creeping juniper) is a prostrate, creeping groundcover. **J. procumbens** (Japanese garden juniper) is a low, wide-spreading shrub. **J. squamata** (singleseed juniper) forms a prostrate or low, spreading shrub or a small, upright tree.

The prickly foliage of junipers gives some gardeners a rash.

Features: foliage; variety of colors, sizes and habits **Habit:** conical or columnar tree, rounded or spreading shrub or prostrate groundcover; evergreen **Height:** 4"–70' **Spread:** 1–48' **Hardiness:** zones 3–8

Katsura Tree

Cercidiphyllum

C. japonicum 'Pendula' (above)
C. japonicum (below)

Katsura tree is native to eastern Asia, and the delicate foliage blends well into Japanese-style gardens.

Katsura tree has exceptional grace and beauty. It is drought sensitive, so watering is recommended during dry periods, especially when the trees are young.

Growing

Katsura tree grows equally well in **full sun** or **partial shade**. The soil should be **fertile, humus rich, neutral to acidic, moist** and **well drained**. This tree establishes more quickly if watered regularly during dry spells for the first year or two.

Tips

Katsura tree works well as a specimen or shade tree. The species is quite large and is best used in large gardens. The cultivar 'Pendula' is quite widespreading but can be used in small gardens.

Recommended

C. japonicum is a slow-growing tree with heart-shaped, blue-green foliage that turns yellow and orange in fall and develops a spicy scent. A **Plant of Merit,** it grows 40–70' tall and wide. **'Pendula'** is one of the most elegant weeping trees available. Usually grafted to a standard, it grows 10–25' tall and wide, and its mounding, cascading branches give the entire tree the appearance of a waterfall tumbling over rocks.

Features: attractive spring, summer and fall foliage; habit; generally pest free
Habit: rounded or spreading, often multi-stemmed, deciduous tree **Height:** 10–70'
Spread: 10–70' or more **Hardiness:** zones 4–8

Lilac
Syringa

Lilacs are very easy to grow, with a large number of species and cultivars from which to choose.

Growing

Lilacs grow best in **full sun**. The soil should be **fertile, humus rich** and **well drained**. These plants tolerate open, windy locations.

Tips

Include lilacs in a shrub or mixed border or use them to create an informal hedge. Japanese tree lilac can be used as a specimen tree.

Recommended

The following list of really good lilacs is severely shortened. Check with your garden center to see what is available.

S. meyeri var. spontanea (Korean lilac) is a compact, rounded shrub that grows 4–8' tall and spreads 6–12'. This **Plant of Merit** bears fragrant, pink or lavender flowers in late spring and early summer and sometimes again in fall. It does not sucker profusely.

S. patula 'Miss Kim' is a hardy lilac with dense branching and very few suckers. It grows 5–10' tall, spreads 3–8' and bears small clusters of fragrant, lilac-colored flowers. The dark green leaves turn burgundy in fall.

S. meyeri var. spontanea (above)
S. vulgaris (below)

Features: late-spring to mid-summer flowers; habit; easy to grow **Habit:** rounded or suckering, deciduous shrub or small tree **Height:** 3–30'
Spread: 3–30' **Hardiness:** zones 3–8

Linden
Tilia

T. cordata (above)

Linden flowers exude a dripping honeydew that coats anything underneath them, so don't plant lindens near a driveway.

Well-proportioned and trouble free, lindens are also among the fastest growing of all large deciduous trees.

Growing
Lindens grow best in **full sun**. The soil should be **average to fertile, moist** and **well drained**. These trees prefer an **alkaline** soil but adapt to most pH levels. *T. cordata* tolerates pollution and urban conditions better than the other lindens listed here.

Tips
Lindens are useful and attractive street trees, shade trees and specimen trees. Their tolerance of pollution and their moderate size make lindens ideal for city gardens.

Recommended
Good cultivars of most species are available.

T. americana (basswood, American linden) is hardy to zone 2; its cultivars are less hardy.

T. cordata (littleleaf linden) is a dense, pyramidal tree that may become rounded with age.

T. tomentosa (silver linden) has a broadly pyramidal or rounded habit that has glossy, green leaves with fuzzy, silvery undersides. It is hardy to zone 4.

Features: fragrant, yellow flowers; habit; foliage **Habit:** dense, pyramidal to rounded, deciduous tree **Height:** 25–80'
Spread: 20–60' **Hardiness:** zones 2–8

Magnolia
Magnolia

Magnolias are magnificent, versatile plants that bear stunningly beautiful, fragrant flowers.

Growing

Magnolias grow well in **full sun** or **partial shade**. The soil should be **fertile, humus rich, acidic, moist** and **well drained**. A summer mulch helps keep the roots cool and the soil moist. *M. virginiana* tolerates wet soil and shade.

Tips

Magnolias are often used as specimen trees. The small species can be used in borders.

Avoid planting magnolias where the morning sun will encourage the blooms to open too early in the season. Cold, wind and rain can damage the blossoms.

Recommended

Many species, hybrids and cultivars are available in a range of sizes and with differing flowering times, flower colors and hardiness zones. The following are **Plant of Merit** selections.

M. grandiflora (southern magnolia) **'Bracken's Brown Beauty'** is reliably evergreen to zone 5b. It is a large, dense, broad, pyramidal to rounded tree that grows 20–30' tall and 15–25' wide and bears fragrant, white flowers.

M. x soulangeana (above)
M. grandiflora hybrid (below)

M. virginiana var. *australis* (sweetbay magnolia) is an evergreen to semi-evergreen, spreading, open shrub or small, multi-stemmed tree. It grows 10–20' tall, with an equal spread, and bears very fragrant, creamy white flowers.

Features: late-spring flowers; fruit; foliage; habit; bark **Habit:** deciduous, upright to spreading shrub or tree **Height:** 10–30' **Spread:** 10–25' **Hardiness:** zones 5–9

Maple
Acer

A. palmatum cultivar (above), *A. griseum* (below)

Maple fruits, called samaras, have wings that act like miniature helicopter rotors and help in seed dispersal.

Maples form a very large group of diverse and varied trees that offer wonderful foliage, stellar form and fiery fall color. They are hardy, problem-resistant, reliable growers.

Growing

Maples generally do well in **full sun** or **light shade,** but species preferences can vary. The soil should be **fertile, moist, high in organic matter** and **well drained**.

Tips

Maples are some of the most popular choices for shade or street trees. They can be used as specimen trees, as large elements in shrub or mixed borders or as hedges. Some are useful as understory plants bordering wooded areas; others can be grown in containers on patios or terraces. Few Japanese gardens are without attractive, small maples. Almost all maples can be used to create bonsai specimens.

Recommended

Many maples are very large when fully mature, but the following small species are useful in small gardens: *A. griseum* (paperbark maple; **Emeritus Plant of Merit**), *A. japonicum* (full moon maple), *A. palmatum* (Japanese maple), *A. truncatum* (purpleblow maple; **Plant of Merit**) and *A. triflorum* (threeflower maple; **Plant of Merit**).

Features: foliage; bark; winged fruit; fall color; form; flowers **Habit:** small, multi-stemmed, deciduous tree or large shrub
Height: 10–30' **Spread:** 10–30'
Hardiness: zones 4–9, varies with species

Ninebark

Physocarpus

P. opulifolius DIABOLO (above & below)

Ninebarks are tough-as-nails plants that feature attractive foliage and colorful early-summer flowers. These easy-growing plants adapt to most conditions.

Growing

Ninebarks grow well in **full sun** (for best leaf coloring) or **partial shade**. The soil should be **fertile, moist** and **well drained**. These shrubs adapt to alkaline soil.

Tips

Easy-to-grow shrubs that adapt to most garden conditions, ninebarks can be included in a shrub or mixed border, in a woodland garden or in a naturalistic garden.

Recommended

P. opulifolius (common ninebark) is a suckering shrub with long, arching branches and exfoliating bark. It bears light pink flowers in early summer and fruit that ripens to reddish green in fall. This Missouri native is a **Plant of Merit**. Several cultivars are available. DIABOLO ('Monlo') has attractive purple foliage.

You may not actually find nine layers, but the peeling, flecked bark of ninebarks does add interest to the winter landscape.

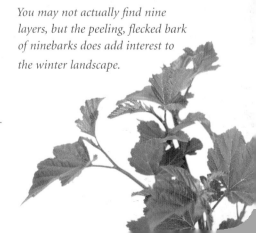

Features: early to mid-summer flowers; fruit; bark; foliage; easy to grow **Habit:** upright, sometimes suckering, deciduous shrub **Height:** 5–10' **Spread:** 5–15' **Hardiness:** zones 2–8

Oak

Quercus

Q. phellos (above)

Take care when watering around oak trees. Do not wet the trunks, especially around the base, to avoid causing internal decay problems.

Mighty oak trees are perfect for large, open parks and gardens. They are adaptable and fast growing, but make sure to give them room to stretch out their branches.

Growing

Oaks grow well in **full sun** or **partial shade**. The soil should be **fertile, moist** and **well drained**. Most oaks prefer slightly acidic soils but adapt to alkaline conditions. Oaks can be difficult to establish; transplant them only while they are young.

Tips

Oaks are large trees that are best as specimens or for groves in parks and large gardens. They are very sensitive to changes in grade and root disturbance, so do not disturb, disrupt or compact the rootzone or the ground around their bases. Keep work areas well back from oaks.

Recommended

There are many oaks to choose from, and only a few popular species are listed here. *Q. alba* (white oak) is a rounded, spreading tree with peeling bark and purplered fall color. *Q. coccinea* (scarlet oak) is an open, rounded tree that has bright red fall color. *Q. phellos* (willow oak) is an open, pyramidal to rounded, graceful, fast-growing **Plant of Merit** with willowlike foliage and yellow fall color.

Features: decorative summer and fall foliage; bark; habit; acorns **Habit:** large, rounded, spreading, deciduous tree **Height:** 40–100' **Spread:** 10–100' **Hardiness:** zones 4–9

Pine

Pinus

The vast *Pinus* genus offers a wide array of interesting landscape plants. With the variety in size and growth forms, there is sure to be a pine for your garden.

Growing

Pines grow best in **full sun**. These trees adapt to most **well-drained** soils but do not tolerate polluted urban conditions.

Tips

Pines are more diverse and widely adapted than any other conifers. Pines can be used as specimen trees, as hedges or to create windbreaks. Small cultivars can be included in shrub or mixed borders. These trees are not heavy feeders; fertilizing encourages rapid new growth that is weak and susceptible to pest and disease problems.

Recommended

Many pines are available, both trees and shrubby dwarf plants. Check with your local garden center or nursery to find out what is available.

P. bungeana (lacebark pine) is a columnar or bushy tree that grows 30–50' tall and spreads 15–35'. This **Plant of Merit** has attractive, exfoliating bark that flakes off in rounded scales, leaving the trunk mottled with patches of cream, brown and red. (Zones 4–8)

P. ponderosa (above), *P. strobus* (below)

The Austrian Pine, *P. nigra*, was often recommended as the most urban-tolerant pine, but overplanting has led to severe disease problems, some of which can kill a tree in a single growing season.

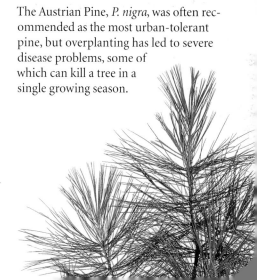

Features: foliage; bark; cones; habit
Habit: upright, columnar, shrubby or spreading, evergreen tree **Height:** 2–120'
Spread: 2–50' **Hardiness:** zones 2–8

Redbud

Cercis

C. canadensis (above & below)

Redbud can be long-lived if the tree's suckers are allowed to develop and replace the original trunk.

This outstanding, native plant is truly a welcome sight in spring. The intense, deep magenta buds open to pink flowers that cover the long, thin branches in clouds of color.

Growing

Redbud grows well in **full sun, partial shade** or **light shade**. The soil should be a **fertile, deep loam** that is **moist** and **well drained**. This plant has tender roots and does not like being transplanted.

Some parts of northern Missouri are close to the northern edge of the range for the native *C. canadensis,* so you may have trouble establishing a young tree if winters are severe. Providing a sheltered location helps.

Tips

Redbud can be used as a specimen tree, in a shrub or mixed border or in a woodland garden.

Select a redbud from a locally grown source. Plants grown from seeds produced in the south are not hardy in the north.

Recommended

C. canadensis (eastern redbud) is a spreading, multi-stemmed tree that bears red, purple or pink flowers. The young foliage is bronze, fading to green over summer and turning bright yellow in fall. Many beautiful cultivars are available. **'Forest Pansy'** is an **Emeritus Plant of Merit** with purple or pink flowers and dark reddish purple foliage that fades to green over summer.

Features: spring flowers; colorful fall foliage
Habit: rounded or spreading, multi-stemmed, deciduous tree or shrub **Height:** 20–30'
Spread: 25–35' **Hardiness:** zones 4–9

Rhododendron · Azalea

Rhododendron

Rhododendrons and azaleas are some of the most beautiful of all flowering shrubs.

Growing

Rhododendrons and evergreen azaleas prefer **partial shade** or **light shade,** but deciduous azaleas perform best in **full sun** or **light shade**. The soil should be **fertile, humus rich, acidic, moist** and **well drained**. These plants are sensitive to high pH, drought, salinity and winter injury. A location **sheltered from strong winds** is preferable. Plants in a protected location should not need burlap covering in winter.

Tips

Rhododendrons and azaleas grow and look better when planted in groups. Use them in shrub or mixed borders, in woodland gardens or in sheltered rock gardens.

Shallow planting with good mulch is essential, as is excellent drainage. To ensure good surface drainage in heavy soils, elevate the crown 1" above soil level when planting.

Recommended

In Missouri, we can grow a number of different rhododendron and azalea species and cultivars.

R. Northern Lights hybrid (above)
Azalea hybrid (below)

R. **'Girard's Rose'** is an upright, evergreen azalea that grows 24–30" tall and wide. It has glossy, dark green foliage that is tinted bronze-red in winter. This **Emeritus Plant of Merit** has deep rose-pink flowers.

R. **Northern Lights hybrids** are broad, rounded, very cold hardy, deciduous azaleas. They grow about 5' tall and 36" wide, with blooms in shades of red, orange, yellow, pink or white.

Rhododendrons and azaleas have shallow roots and resent being disturbed.

Features: late-winter to early-summer flowers; foliage; habit **Habit:** upright, mounding, rounded, evergreen or deciduous shrub **Height:** 1–10' **Spread:** 2–10' **Hardiness:** zones 4–8

River Birch
Betula

When it comes to showy bark, river birch is unmatched. The attractive, peeling bark adds a whole new dimension to the garden.

Growing
River birch grows well in **full sun, partial shade** or **light shade,** in **neutral to slightly acidic, moist, fairly well-drained** soil of **average fertility**. River birch tolerates occasional flooding and wet soils.

Tips
Birch trees are often used as specimens. Their small leaves and open canopy provide light shade that allows perennials, annuals and lawns to flourish below. If you have enough space, birches look attractive when grown in groups near natural or artificial water features.

Recommended
B. nigra (black birch, red birch) has shaggy, cinnamon brown bark that flakes off in sheets when the tree is young, but the bark thickens and becomes more ridged as the tree matures. This species is resistant to pests and diseases. DURA-HEAT ('BNMTF') can really handle our Missouri heat. The densely packed, small, glossy, dark green leaves resist leaf spot and turn a nice yellow in fall. HERITAGE ('Cully') is a vigorous grower that resists leaf spot and heat stress. An **Emeritus Plant of Merit,** it has larger, glossier leaves than the species. The bark begins peeling when the tree is quite young.

Features: attractive foliage and bark; fall color; winter and spring catkins **Habit:** open, single or multi-stemmed, deciduous tree **Height:** 40–70' **Spread:** 30–50' **Hardiness:** zones 3–9

B. nigra (above & below)

Serviceberry
Amelanchier

These tough, easy-to-grow shrubs are beautiful in informal mass plantings, and they can be absolutely stunning in formal settings.

Growing
Serviceberries grow well in **full sun** or **light shade**. They prefer **acidic** soil that is **fertile, humus rich, moist** and **well drained**, but they do adjust to drought. *A. canadensis* tolerates boggy soil conditions.

Tips
Serviceberries make beautiful specimen plants or even shade trees in small gardens. The shrubby forms can be grown along the edges of a woodland or in a border. In the wild, these trees are often found growing near water sources, and they are beautiful beside ponds or streams.

Recommended
The following species have white spring flowers, purple fruit and good fall color.

*A. **arborea*** (common serviceberry, June-berry, downy serviceberry) is a **Plant of Merit**. The medium green foliage of this small, single- or multi-stemmed tree turns shades of yellow to red in fall.

*A. **x grandiflora*** (apple serviceberry) is a small, spreading, often multi-stemmed tree. The new foliage is often bronzy, turning green in summer and bright orange or red in fall. **'Autumn Brilliance'** is a fast-growing **Plant of Merit** selection with leaves that turn brilliant red in fall.

A. arborea (above & below)

Serviceberry fruit can be used in place of blueberries in any recipe. The fruit has a similar but generally sweeter flavor.

Also called: saskatoon, Juneberry, shadberry
Features: spring or early-summer flowers; edible fruit; fall color; habit; bark
Habit: single- or multi-stemmed, deciduous, large shrub or small tree **Height:** 15–30'
Spread: 15–30' **Hardiness:** zones 4–9

Smokebush

Cotinus

C. coggygria (above & below)

Smokebush is an excellent, easy-to-grow addition to the garden. It has showy flowers, attractive summer foliage and good fall color, and it adapts to poor, dry soils.

Growing

Smokebush grows well in **full sun** or **partial shade**. It prefers soil of **average fertility** that is **moist** and **well drained**. Established plants adapt to dry, sandy soils. Smokebush is very tolerant of alkaline, gravelly soil.

Smokebush's many-branched flower clusters, usually dull purple and hairy, produce the effect of puffs of smoke above the foliage.

Tips

Smokebush can be used in a shrub or mixed border, as a single specimen or in groups. It is a good choice for a rocky hillside planting.

Recommended

C. coggygria is a bushy, rounded shrub that develops large, puffy plumes of flowers that start out green and gradually turn pinky gray. The green foliage turns red, orange and yellow in fall. Many cultivars are available. **'Royal Purple'** (purple smokebush) has purplish red flowers and dark purple foliage. **'Velvet Cloak'** is a **Plant of Merit** selection with purple flowers. It has deep purple foliage with a reddish purple fall color.

Features: early-summer flowers; decorative summer and fall foliage; easy to grow **Habit:** bushy, rounded, spreading, deciduous tree or shrub **Height:** 8–15' **Spread:** 8–15' **Hardiness:** zones 4–8

Spicebush
Lindera

Named for the spicy scent of the stems when bruised, this native shrub deserves to be more widely used in our gardens.

Growing
Spicebush grows best in **light** or **partial shade,** but it tolerates full sun. The soil should be **fertile, acidic, moist** and **well drained**.

Tips
The habit of spicebush varies depending on how much sun it receives; it can be quite relaxed and open in shaded locations but becomes denser in sunnier situations. Spicebush makes a lovely addition to moist, open woodland gardens in spots where the tiny but plentiful, greenish yellow flowers can be enjoyed in early spring.

Recommended
L. benzoin is a rounded, dense to open, multi-stemmed, deciduous shrub. This **Plant of Merit** selection bears greenish yellow flowers in mid-spring, followed by red berries in summer. The fragrant, dark green foliage turns an incandescent yellow in fall.

L. benzoin (above & below)

The scarlet fruit of spicebush is one of the few berries that contains fat, which is needed by migrating and overwintering birds.

Features: fragrant stems and leaves; greenish yellow mid-spring flowers; fall color
Height: 6–12' **Spread:** 6–12'
Hardiness: zones 4–9

Spruce
Picea

P. glauca 'Conica' (above)
P. pungens var. glauca 'Moerheim' (below)

Spruces are among the most commonly grown evergreens. Plant spruces where they have enough room to allow the branches to reach all the way to the ground.

Oil-based pesticides, such as dormant oil, can take the blue out of your blue-needled spruces.

Growing

Spruce trees grow best in **full sun**. Dwarf Alberta spruces prefer **light shade** and a sheltered location. The soil should be **neutral to acidic, deep** and **well drained**. Spruces tolerate alkaline soils, but they generally don't like hot, dry or polluted conditions. Spruces are best grown from small, young stock because they dislike being transplanted when larger or more mature.

Tips

Spruce trees add an element of formality to the garden, and they are mostly used as specimens. The dwarf and slow-growing cultivars can also be used in shrub or mixed borders. These trees look most attractive when allowed to keep their lower branches.

Recommended

Spruces are generally upright, pyramidal trees, but cultivars may be low-growing, wide-spreading or even weeping in habit. *P. abies* (Norway spruce), *P. glauca* (white spruce), *P. pungens* (Colorado spruce) and their cultivars are popular and commonly available. **'Fat Albert'** is a **Plant of Merit**. It is a dense, cone-shaped tree with ascending branches and steel blue needles. It typically grows 10–15' tall and 7–10' wide.

Features: foliage; cones; habit
Habit: conical or columnar, evergreen tree or shrub **Height:** 3–80' **Spread:** 2–25'
Hardiness: zones 2–8

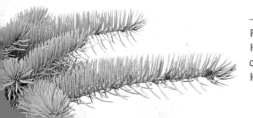

Sumac

Rhus

R. typhina (above), *R. aromatica* (below)

Sumacs are attractive, easy-to-grow, long-lived, spreading plants.

Growing

Sumacs develop the best fall color in **full sun** but tolerate partial shade. The soil should be of **average fertility, moist** and **well drained**. Once established, sumacs are very drought tolerant.

These plants can become invasive. Remove suckers that come up where you don't want them.

Tips

Sumacs can be used in a shrub or mixed border, in a woodland garden or on a sloping bank. Both male and female plants are needed for fruit to form.

Recommended

R. aromatica (fragrant sumac) forms a low mound of suckering stems 2–6' tall and 5–10' wide. The aromatic foliage turns red or purple in fall. **'Gro-Low'** is an **Emeritus Plant of Merit** groundcover that grows 24" tall and 8' wide. (Zones 3–9)

R. copallina (shining sumac, flameleaf sumac) has exotic, shiny foliage with "wings" on the leaf stalks between the leaflets. The foliage turns crimson in fall. This shrub grows 12' tall and wide.

R. typhina (staghorn sumac) is a suckering, colony-forming shrub that grows 15–25' tall and spreads 25' or more. The leaves turn stunning shades of yellow, orange and red in fall.

Features: attractive summer and fall foliage; chartreuse summer flowers; fuzzy, red fall fruit; habit **Habit:** bushy, suckering, colony-forming, deciduous shrub **Height:** 2–25'
Spread: 5–25' or more; often exceeds height
Hardiness: zones 4–9

Summersweet Clethra
Clethra

C. alnifolia 'Hummingbird' (above), *C. alnifolia* cultivar (below)

Summersweet clethra attracts butterflies and other pollinators and is one of the best shrubs for adding fragrance to your garden. It doesn't like it dry, so make sure to give it a little extra water.

Growing
Summersweet clethra grows best in **light** or **partial shade**. The soil should be **fertile, humus rich, acidic, moist** and **well drained,** but poorly drained organic soils are tolerated.

Summersweet clethra is useful in damp, shaded gardens, where the late-season flowers are much appreciated.

Tips
Although not aggressive, this shrub tends to sucker, forming a colony of stems. Use it in a border or in a woodland garden. The light shade along the edge of a woodland is an ideal location. The dwarf cultivars are great at the front of a border.

Recommended
C. alnifolia is a large, rounded, upright, colony-forming shrub that bears attractive spikes of highly fragrant, white flowers. The foliage turns yellow in fall. **'Hummingbird'** is compact and low growing. **'Pink Spires'** ('Rosea') is a large plant that bears pink flowers. **'Ruby Spice'** bears fade-resistant, deep pink flowers. **'September Beauty'** bears large, white flowers later in the season than other selections.

Also called: sweet pepperbush, sweetspire
Features: fragrant summer flowers; attractive habit; colorful fall foliage **Habit:** rounded, suckering, deciduous shrub **Height:** 2–8'
Spread: 2–8' **Hardiness:** zones 3–9

Sweetspire
Itea

Sweetspire is valued for the fragrance that emanates from the showy, elongated bottlebrush flower clusters. Vibrant fall color is another reason to use sweetspire.

Growing

Sweetspire grows well in all light conditions from **full sun** (best fall color) **to full shade** (less arching, more upright habit). The soil should be **fertile** and **moist,** although sweetspire is fairly adaptable. Chlorosis (leaf yellowing) may occur in highly alkaline soils or during drought.

Tips

Sweetspire is an excellent shrub for low-lying and moist areas. It grows well near streams and water features. It is also a fine choice for plantings in areas where the scent of the fragrant flowers can be enjoyed. Sweetspire can be used individually or in small groups in the home garden, and it looks awesome mass planted in large areas.

Recommended

I. virginica is an upright to arching, suckering shrub that usually grows wider than tall. Spikes of fragrant, white flowers appear in late spring, and the leaves turn shades of purple and red in fall. **'Henry's Garnet'** is an **Emeritus Plant of Merit**. It bears larger and more flower spikes and has consistently better dark red-purple fall color than the species. **'Sprich'** (LITTLE HENRY) is a compact cultivar with bright red fall color.

I. virginica 'Henry's Garnet' (above)
I. virginica (below)

Sweetspire has been refined from its wild, straggly habit, and recent cultivars offer neat, compact additions to the shrub border.

Features: attractive habit; fragrant flowers; fall color **Habit:** upright to arching, deciduous shrub **Height:** 2–6' **Spread:** 3–6' or more **Hardiness:** zones: 5–9

Viburnum

Viburnum

V. opulus (above)
V. plicatum var. tomentosum (below)

Many species of birds are attracted to viburnums.

Viburnums are a large, versatile, diverse group of low-maintenance shrubs that come in many shapes and sizes and offer multi-season interest. Include at least one viburnum in your landscape, and you will not be disappointed.

Growing

Viburnums grow well in **full sun, partial shade** or **light shade**. The soil should be of **average fertility, moist** and **well drained**. Viburnums tolerate both alkaline and acidic soils.

Deadheading keeps these plants looking neat, but it also prevents fruits from forming. Fruiting is better when more than one plant of a species is grown.

Tips

Viburnums can be used in borders and woodland gardens. They are a good choice for plantings near swimming pools.

Recommended

Many viburnum species, hybrids and cultivars are available. A few popular ones are listed here. *V. carlesii* (Korean spice viburnum) is a dense, bushy, rounded, deciduous shrub with spicy-scented, white or pink flowers. *V. opulus* (European cranberrybush, guelder-rose) is a rounded, spreading, deciduous shrub with lacy-looking flower clusters. *V. plicatum* var. *tomentosum* (doublefile viburnum) has a graceful, horizontal branching pattern that gives the shrub a layered effect and lacy-looking, white flower clusters.

Features: flowers (some fragrant); decorative summer and fall foliage; fruit; habit **Habit:** bushy or spreading, evergreen, semi-evergreen or deciduous shrub **Height:** 2–20' **Spread:** 2–15' **Hardiness:** zones 2–9

Weigela
Weigela

The impressive, long-lasting bloom of weigelas is reason enough to include them in your garden. The bright, trumpet-shaped flowers attract attention and hummingbirds.

Growing

Weigelas prefer **full sun** or **partial shade,** depending on the variety; for the best leaf color, grow purple-leaved plants in full sun and yellow-leaved plants in partial shade. The soil should be **fertile** and **well drained,** although weigelas adapt to most well-drained soils.

Tips

Weigelas can be used in shrub or mixed borders, in open woodland gardens or as informal barrier plantings.

Recommended

W. florida is a spreading shrub with arching branches that bears clusters of dark pink flowers. Many hybrids and cultivars are available, including dwarf varieties, red-, pink- or white-flowered selections and plants with purple, bronze or yellow foliage. MIDNIGHT WINE ('Elvera') is a dwarf plant with purple foliage and pink flowers. WINE AND ROSES ('Alexandra') has dark purple foliage and vivid pink flowers.

W. **'Olympiade'** (BRIANT RUBIDOR) is a **Plant of Merit**. It is a dense, rounded to spreading shrub that grows about 6' tall and wide. The new foliage is green, but it quickly changes to bright yellow or yellow-green with yellow margins. This plant has wonderfully contrasting deep red flowers.

W. florida WINE & ROSES ('Alexandra') (above)
W. florida (below)

Weigelas are one of the longest-blooming shrubs, with the main flush of blooms lasting as long as six weeks. They often re-bloom if sheared lightly after the first flowers fade.

Features: late-spring to early-summer flowers; foliage; habit **Habit:** upright or low, spreading, deciduous shrub **Height:** 1–9' **Spread:** 2–12' **Hardiness:** zones 3–8

Witch Hazel

Hamamelis

H. virginiana (above & below)

H. vernalis is a medium-sized, native shrub found in the wild across Missouri, a good indication that the same plant purchased at the nursery likely requires little special care in your garden.

Growing

Witch hazel grows best in a **sheltered** spot with **full sun** or **light shade**. The soil should be of **average fertility, neutral to acidic, moist** and **well drained**.

Tips

Witch hazel works well individually or in groups. It can be used as a specimen plant, in shrub or mixed borders or in woodland gardens. *H. x intermedia* is ideal as a small tree for space-limited gardens.

The unique flowers have long, narrow, crinkled petals. If the weather gets too cold, the petals roll up, protecting the flowers and extending the flowering season.

Recommended

H. x intermedia is a vase-shaped, spreading shrub that grows 6–20' tall and 8–15' wide, and it bears fragrant clusters of yellow, orange or red flowers in early spring. The leaves turn attractive shades of orange, red and bronze in fall. Cultivars are available. (Zones 5–9)

H. vernalis (Ozark witch hazel, vernal witch hazel) is a rounded, upright, often suckering shrub, 6–10' tall and 8–15' wide, with very fragrant, early-spring flowers. It is a **Plant of Merit** and is native to Missouri. (Zones 4–8)

Features: fragrant flowers; decorative summer and fall foliage; habit **Habit:** spreading, deciduous shrub or small tree **Height:** 6–20' **Spread:** 6–15' **Hardiness:** zones 4–9

Carefree Beauty

Modern Shrub Rose

This magnificent rose was developed by the late Dr. Griffith J. Buck at Iowa State University. It is one in the long line of Dr. Buck's "prairie" show-stoppers, which are perfectly suited to Missouri gardens.

Growing

Carefree Beauty requires a location in **full sun**. **Organically rich, slightly acidic, well-drained** soil is best, but this shrub rose can tolerate slight shade and poorer soils.

Tips

This upright shrub's spreading habit makes it an ideal candidate for a low-maintenance hedge. It also makes a fine specimen, and it will complement other flowering shrubs and perennials in mixed borders.

Recommended

Rosa 'Carefree Beauty' bears small clusters of 4½" wide, semi-double, deep pink blossoms, not once but twice throughout the growing season. The large size of the blossoms compensates for the small number at the end of each stem. The fragrant flowers beautifully complement the smooth, olive green foliage. Orange-red hips add interest from winter until early spring.

Features: large, fragrant, deep pink blossoms; disease-free foliage; vigorous growth habit
Height: 5–6' **Spread:** 4–5'
Hardiness: zones 3–9

Carefree Delight

Modern Shrub Rose

The name of this shrub rose is perfectly appropriate—it requires very little care and produces copious quantities of flowers in waves throughout summer.

Growing

Carefree Delight prefers **full sun** but tolerates some shade. The soil should be **average to fertile, humus rich, slightly acidic, moist** and **well drained,** but this rose has proven to be quite adaptable to a variety of soil conditions. Carefree Delight is disease resistant.

Carefree Delight is consistent in all climates, making it suitable for just about any setting or region.

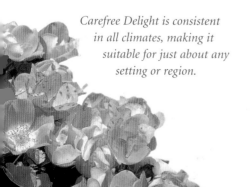

Tips

Carefree Delight makes a good addition to a mixed bed or border, and it is attractive when planted in groups of three or more. It can be mass planted to create a large display or grown singly as an equally attractive specimen.

Recommended

Rosa 'Carefree Delight' is a bushy, rounded shrub with glossy, dark green foliage that turns bronzy red in fall. Large clusters of single, pink flowers with white or yellow centers and contrasting yellow stamens are borne for most of summer. There are several other roses in the **Carefree Series,** including '**Carefree Beauty'** (see p. 109) and '**Carefree Sunshine,'** which bears yellow flowers.

Features: rounded habit; decorative summer and fall foliage; long blooming period; attractive hips; disease resistant; carmine pink flowers with white or yellow centers **Height:** 3–4' **Spread:** 3–4' **Hardiness:** zones 4–9

Cécile Brünner

Polyantha Rose

This beloved old-timer is much admired for its small, classically shaped blooms that appear almost continuously from early summer to fall.

Growing

Cécile Brünner prefers **full sun** and **fertile, humus-rich, slightly acidic, moist, well-drained** soil.

Tips

Cécile Brünner works well when used in mixed beds and borders or as part of a foundation planting. It also does great in containers.

Recommended

Rosa **"Cécile Brünner"** is a small plant with upright stems and sparse, disease-resistant, dark green foliage. This long-lived variety with almost thorn-less stems bears urn-shaped, fully double, light pink flowers that have a sweet, slightly spicy fragrance. It blooms from early summer to fall, prolifically at first, then sporadically. A vigor-ous climbing form that grows 20' tall and wide is also available.

Because it frequently adorned buttonholes in the early 1900s, Cécile Brünner was often called the "boutonniere rose."

Also called: sweetheart rose, Maltese rose, mignon **Features:** repeat to almost continuous blooming; light pink flowers **Height:** 24–36" **Spread:** 24" **Hardiness:** zones 5–9

Dortmund

Climbing Rose

Few roses are rated as highly and respected as much as Dortmund. The foliage alone makes it worth growing.

Growing

Plant Dortmund in **full sun,** in **fertile, humus-rich, slightly acidic, moist, well-drained** soil. Dortmund requires reasonably good growing conditions to thrive, but it tolerates light, dappled shade and poorer soils and is highly disease resistant.

Deadhead heavily and frequently to encourage blooming. Discontinue dead-heading at least five weeks before the first fall frost to allow the plant to form a large crop of bright red hips in fall.

Tips

This rose can grow large enough to cover one side of a small building. To create a medium shrub useful for hedging or as a specimen, prune to control the size. As a climber, it can be trained up a pillar, veranda post, wall or trellis. It can also be grafted as a weeping standard.

Recommended

Rosa **'Dortmund'** is a tall, upright plant with dense, glossy, dark green foliage. Dortmund blooms from spring to fall, with the majority of flowers occurring in spring. Blooming is a little slow to start, but once it begins to take off, the results are worth the wait. The flowers have a light apple scent, and each large, red flower has a glowing central white eye and bright yellow stamens.

Features: attractive foliage and habit; abundant white-eyed, red flowers; repeat blooming **Height:** 14–24' **Spread:** 8–10' **Hardiness:** zones 5–9

Flower Carpet
Groundcover Rose

Since their release in 1991, FLOWER CARPET roses have proven themselves to be low-maintenance, black spot-resistant, long-blooming performers in the landscape.

Growing

FLOWER CARPET roses grow best in **full sun**. The soil should be **average to fertile, humus rich, slightly acidic, moist** and **well drained**, but this hardy rose is fairly adaptable.

Tips

Although not true groundcovers, these small shrub roses have dense and spreading habits useful for filling in large areas. They can also be used as low hedges or in mixed borders. The sometimes long, rangy canes may require some pruning to reduce their spread. FLOWER CARPET roses grow well even near roads, sidewalks or driveways where salt is applied in winter.

Recommended

Rosa FLOWER CARPET roses are bushy, low-growing, spreading plants with leathery, shiny, bright green foliage. They produce single or semi-double flowers in colors designated white, yellow, pink, coral, red or apple blossom, with prominent yellow stamens. These flowers last from early summer through fall to the first heavy frost.

Features: mounding, spreading habit; deep hot pink, white, yellow, coral, red or apple blossom flowers from summer through fall
Height: 30–36" **Spread:** 3–4'
Hardiness: zones 5–9

Iceberg
Floribunda Rose

Over 40 years have passed since this exceptional rose was first introduced into commerce, and its continued popularity proves it can stand the test of time.

Growing

Iceberg grows best in **full sun**. The soil should be **fertile, humus rich, slightly acidic, moist** and **well drained**. Winter protection may be required in the northern parts of the state. Deadhead to prolong blooming.

Tips

Iceberg is a popular addition to mixed borders and beds, and it also works well as a specimen. Plant it in a well-used area or near a window, where its flower fragrance can best be enjoyed. This rose can also be included in large planters or patio containers.

Recommended

Rosa 'Iceberg' is a vigorous shrub with a rounded, bushy habit and light green foliage. It produces clusters of semi-double flowers in several flushes from early summer to fall. A climbing variation of this rose is reputed to be the best climbing white rose ever developed.

Climbing Iceberg, a sport of Iceberg, is easily trained on small fences, pergolas, arches, pillars and veranda posts. It is considered one of the best white climbing roses available, bearing disease-resistant foliage on almost thornless stems.

Also called: Fée des Neiges **Features:** bushy habit; strong, sweet fragrance; white flowers, sometimes flushed with pink during cool or wet weather, from early summer to fall
Height: 3–4' **Spread:** 3–4'
Hardiness: zones 5–8

Knock Out

Modern Shrub Rose

Knock Out series roses are tough and disease resistant, and they bloom almost continuously. Knock Out has been called "perhaps the best-ever landscape rose for four-season interest."

Growing

Knock Out grows best in **full sun**. The soil should be **fertile, humus rich, slightly acidic, moist** and **well drained**. This rose blooms most prolifically in warm weather but has deeper red flowers in cooler weather. Deadhead lightly to keep the plant tidy and to encourage prolific blooming.

Tips

This vigorous rose makes a good addition to a mixed bed or border and is attractive when planted in groups of three or more. It can be mass planted to create a large display or grown singly as an equally beautiful specimen.

Recommended

Rosa 'Knock Out' has a lovely, rounded form with glossy, green leaves that turn to shades of burgundy in fall. The bright, cherry red flowers, in clusters of 3–15, are borne almost all summer and in early fall. Orange-red hips last well into winter. Available cultivars include a light pink selection called 'Blushing Knock Out,' as well as 'Double Knock Out' and 'Pink Knock Out.' All have excellent disease resistance.

Features: rounded habit; lightly tea rose–scented, mid-summer to fall flowers in shades of pink and red; disease resistant **Height:** 3–4' **Spread:** 3–4' **Hardiness:** zones 4–10

New Dawn
Climbing Rose

New Dawn is one of the all-time favorite climbing varieties among gardeners and rosarians. In 1910, Dr. William Van Fleet of the United States introduced a hybrid seedling named "Dr. W. Van Fleet"; it gave rise to a repeat-blooming sport introduced in 1930 as "The New Dawn."

Growing
New Dawn grows well in **full sun** or **partial shade,** in **fertile, moist, well-drained** soil with at least **5% organic matter** mixed in.

Tips
Considered one of the easiest climbers to grow, this rose is suitable for pergolas, walls, fences, arches or pillars, or it can be pruned as a hedge or shrub. It is also a good rose for exhibition.

Recommended
Rosa '**New Dawn**' is a vigorous, disease-resistant climber with upright, arching canes that support abundant shiny, medium to dark green leaves. Borne in small clusters or singly, the double flowers have a sweet apple fragrance and fade from a soft pink to a pinkish white.

During their 1997 Triennial Convention, members of the World Federation of Rose Societies elected New Dawn into the Hall of Fame. It was celebrated as the world's first patented plant.

Also called: Everblooming Dr. W. Van Fleet, The New Dawn **Features:** pale pearl pink flowers from early summer to fall; repeat blooming; climbing habit **Height:** 15–20' **Spread:** 10–15' **Hardiness:** zones 5–9

The Fairy

Modern Shrub Rose

The Fairy is popular with novice and experienced gardeners. It bears large clusters of dainty, rosette-shaped, double, soft pink flowers.

Growing

The Fairy grows well in **full sun** or **partial shade;** flower color fades more slowly in partial shade, but black spot is more likely. It prefers **fertile, moist, well-drained** soil with at least **5% organic matter** mixed in. Roses can tolerate light breezes, but keep them out of strong winds. They are heavy feeders and drinkers, and they do not like to share their root space with other plants.

The Fairy doesn't just tolerate neglect, it prefers it.

Tips

This rose can be used in containers, as a groundcover, in mixed beds and borders or as a weeping standard, or it can be left to trail over a low wall or embankment. It looks great massed or planted as low hedging. It also makes a beautiful cut flower.

Recommended

Rosa **'The Fairy'** is a compact, mounding plant with moderately prickly canes and glossy foliage. It is trouble free and highly resistant to disease. It blooms continually until fall frost.

Also called: Fairy, Feerie **Features:** soft pink, repeat blooming, late summer to fall flowers; low maintenance **Height:** 24"
Spread: 2–4' **Hardiness:** zones 4–9

Zéphrine Drouhin
Old Garden Rose—Bourbon

Because of the lack of prickles on its stems and the wonderfully fragrant flowers, Zéphrine Drouhin is an excellent rose for growing next to walkways and entrances.

Growing

Zéphrine Drouhin grows well in **full sun** and tolerates partial shade. The soil should be **fertile, moist** and **well drained,** with at least **5% organic matter** mixed in. Roses can tolerate light breezes, but keep them out of strong winds. They are heavy feeders and drinkers, and they do not like to share their root space with other plants.

Tips

This rose performs well when planted as a hedge or when trained to climb over archways, pergolas or other garden structures.

Recommended

Rosa 'Zéphrine Drouhin' is a vigorous, large, open shrub with prickle-free canes and semi-glossy, medium green foliage. It bears fragrant, semi-double, pink flowers in early summer with good repeat blooming. It is prone to black spot in areas with poor air circulation.

On roses, what we usually refer to as thorns are really prickles, defined botanically as small, thin, sharp outgrowths of the young bark, whereas thorns are sharp outgrowths from the wood of the stem.

Also called: The Thornless Rose
Features: medium to deep pink, repeat blooming, early summer flowers; easy to grow
Height: 8–14' **Spread:** 6–8'
Hardiness: zones 6–9

Black-Eyed Susan Vine

Thunbergia

Black-eyed Susan vine is a useful plant dotted with simple flowers, giving it a cheerful, welcoming appearance.

Growing

Black-eyed Susan vine does well in **full sun, partial shade** or **light shade**. Grow it in **fertile, evenly moist, well-drained** soil that is **high in organic matter**.

This perennial vine is treated as an annual. It can be quite vigorous and may need to be trimmed back from time to time.

Tips

Black-eyed Susan vine can be trained to twine up and around fences, walls, trees and shrubs. It is also attractive trailing down from the top of a rock garden or rock wall or growing in a mixed container or hanging basket.

Recommended

T. alata is a vigorous, twining climber. It bears yellow flowers, often with dark centers, in summer and fall. Cultivars with large flowers in yellow, orange or white are available.

T. alata (above & below)

The blooms of black-eyed Susan vine are trumpet-shaped, with the dark centers forming a tube.

Features: twining habit; dark-centered, yellow or orange flowers **Height:** 5' or more **Spread:** equal to height, if trained **Hardiness:** tender perennial treated as an annual

Clematis
Clematis

C. x jackmanii 'Rubra' (above)
C. 'Gravetye Beauty' (below)

Clematis plants are fast-growing, climbing vines that cover themselves with large, beautiful blooms. With so many clematis to choose from, it is possible to have one in bloom all season.

Growing

Clematis vines prefer **full sun** but tolerate partial shade. The soil should be **fertile, humus rich, moist** and **well drained**. They enjoy warm, sunny weather but prefer cool roots. A thick layer of mulch or a planting of low, shade-providing perennials protects the tender roots. Clematis are quite cold hardy but fare best when protected from winter wind. The rootball should be planted about 2" beneath the soil surface.

Tips

Clematis vines can climb up structures such as trellises, railings, fences and arbors. They can also be allowed to grow over shrubs and up trees or can be used as groundcover.

Recommended

There are many species, hybrids and cultivars of clematis. The flower forms, blooming times and plant sizes can vary.

C. **x jackmanii** (Jackman clematis) is a mid- to late summer bloomer that grows about 10' tall and bears large, purple flowers.

C. **'Nelly Moser'** is an early-summer bloomer that grows about 10' tall. It bears pale mauve-pink flowers with a darker pink stripe down the center of each petal.

C. **'Will Goodwin'** bears large, pale lavender-blue flowers with wavy petals in early to mid-summer. This twining vine grows about 10' tall.

Also called: virgin's bower **Features:** twining habit; blue, purple, pink, yellow, red or white flowers in early to late summer; decorative seedheads **Height:** 8–12' **Spread:** 2–4' **Hardiness:** zones 4–8

Climbing Hydrangea

Hydrangea

H. anomala subsp. *petiolaris* (above & below)

A mature climbing hydrangea can cover an entire wall. With its dark, glossy leaves and delicate, lacy flowers, it is quite possibly one of the most stunning climbing plants available.

Growing

Climbing hydrangea grows well in **full sun** or **partial shade** (shade or partial shade reduces leaf and flower scorch in the hot regions). The soil should be of **average to high fertility, humus rich, moist** and **well drained**. This plant performs best in cool, moist conditions.

Tips

Climbing hydrangea climbs up trees, walls, fences, pergolas and arbors. It clings to walls by means of aerial roots, so it needs no support, just a somewhat textured surface. Climbing hydrangea also grows over rocks, or it can be used as a groundcover or trained to form a small tree or shrub.

Recommended

H. anomala subsp. ***petiolaris*** (*H. petiolaris*) is a clinging vine with glossy, dark green leaves that sometimes turn an attractive yellow in fall. For more than a month in mid-summer, the vine is covered with white, lacy-looking flowers, and the entire plant appears to be veiled in a lacy mist. Most flowers are produced when this **Plant of Merit** is exposed to some direct sunlight each day.

Considered the Cadillac of vines, climbing hydrangea is especially beautiful when grown up a tall, high-limbed tree.

Features: flowers; clinging habit; exfoliating bark **Height:** 50–80' **Spread:** 50–80'
Hardiness: zones 4–9

Dutchman's Pipe
Aristolochia

A. macrophylla (above & below)

$\mathcal{I}$f exotic, unusual, vigorous climb-ers are what you're looking for, then look no further than a Dutchman's pipe. These plants also bear unusual, pipe-shaped flowers, although they are often hidden behind dense curtains of large, heart-shaped leaves.

Growing
Dutchman's pipes grow well in **full sun or partial shade, in fertile, well-drained soil.** Provide a sturdy support for the vines to twine up. They can be cut back as needed during the growing season and should be thinned to a strong frame of main branches in late fall or spring. The vines die back in winter, and mulching for added protection is a must.

Tips
Duchman's pipes are grown on trellises, arbors and buildings for quick-growing screens.

Recommended
A. macrophylla (*A. durior;* smooth Dutchman's pipe) is a deciduous, twin-ing vine that bears unusual, pipe-shaped, green flowers with brown, purple and yellow mottling. Some people find the scent of the flowers unpleasant.

A. tomentosa (woolly Dutchman's pipe) is native to Missouri and is a **Plant of Merit**. It has dark green foliage in abun-dance, and the whole plant is hairy, including the foliage, stems and yellow-green flowers.

Butterflies adore the flowers of Dutchman's pipes.

Features: unusual, exotic flowers; heart-shaped leaves; twining habit; pollinating insect attractant **Height:** 20–30' **Spread:** 5–10' **Hardiness:** zones 5–8

Hardy Kiwi
Actinidia

Hardy kiwis are handsome, useful, vigorous vines. Featuring attractive foliage and adaptability, they are great for difficult sites.

Growing
Hardy kiwi vines grow best in **full sun,** but they also grow well in **partial shade**. The soil should be **fertile** and **well drained**. These plants require **shelter** from strong winds.

Hardy kiwi vines can grow uncontrollably. Don't be afraid to prune them back if they are getting out of hand.

Tips
These vines need a sturdy structure to twine around. Pergolas, arbors and sufficiently large and sturdy fences provide good support. Given a trellis against a wall, a tree or some other upright structure, hardy kiwis twine upward all summer. They can also be grown in containers.

Recommended
Two hardy kiwi vines are commonly grown in Missouri gardens.

A. arguta (hardy kiwi, bower actinidia) has heart-shaped, dark green leaves, white flowers and edible, smooth-skinned, greenish yellow fruit.

A. kolomikta (variegated kiwi vine, kolomikta actinidia) has green leaves strongly variegated with pink and white, white flowers and edible, smooth-skinned, greenish yellow fruit.

A. kolomikta (above), A. arguta (below)

Both a male and a female vine must be present for fruit to be produced, so hardy kiwi vines are often sold in pairs.

Features: early-summer flowers; edible fruit; twining habit **Height:** 15–30' **Spread:** 15–30' **Hardiness:** zones 3–8

Honeysuckle
Lonicera

Honeysuckles are long-lived, vigorous, twining vines that boast colorful, often fragrant flowers. Choose a spot where your honeysuckle can be enjoyed without running rampant over its neighbors.

Growing
Honeysuckles grow well in **full sun** and tolerate partial shade. The soil should be **average to fertile, humus rich, moist** and **well drained**.

Tips
Honeysuckle vines are twining, deciduous climbers that can be trained to grow up a trellis, fence, arbor or other structure. They can spread as widely as they climb to fill the space provided.

Recommended
L. x *heckrottii* (goldflame honeysuckle) is a deciduous to semi-evergreen vine with attractive blue-green foliage. It bears fragrant, pink or yellow flowers.

L. sempervirens (above), *L. x heckrottii* (below)

L. sempervirens (trumpet honeysuckle, coral honeysuckle) bears orange or red flowers. Many cultivars are available, with flowers in yellow, red or scarlet.

Choosing the right honeysuckle, planting it in the proper site and pruning it regularly make all the difference in enjoying these plants.

Features: orange, red, yellow or pink flowers in spring, summer or fall; twining habit; fruit
Height: 10–20' **Spread:** 10–20'
Hardiness: zones 3–8

Hyacinth Bean
Lablab (Dolichos)

L. purpureus (above & below)

Hyacinth bean is a great vine for providing quick cover. The purple flowers and iridescent, purple seed pods are a delight. The dark green foliage really complements the purple flowers.

Growing
Hyacinth bean prefers **full sun**. The soil should be **average to fertile, moist** and **well drained**. Feed regularly to encourage plentiful flowering. Direct sow the seeds around the predicted last frost date, or start them indoors in peat pots in early spring.

Tips
Hyacinth bean needs a trellis, net, pole or other structure to twine up. Plant it against a fence or near a balcony. If you grow it as a groundcover, make sure it doesn't engulf smaller plants.

Recommended
L. purpureus (*Dolichos lablab*) is a vigorously twining vine. This **Plant of Merit** selection can grow up to 30' tall, but it grows only about 10–15' tall when grown as an annual. It bears many purple or white flowers over summer; they are followed by deep purple pods.

The purple pods of hyacinth bean contain a cyanide-releasing chemical when raw, so eat them only if thoroughly cooked with two to four changes of water.

Also called: Egyptian bean, lablab bean, lablab, Indian bean **Features:** large, bold leaves; habit; sweet-pea–like, purple or white flowers; purple seed pods **Height:** 10–15' **Spread:** variable **Hardiness:** grown as an annual

Japanese Hydrangea Vine
Schizophragma

S. *hydrangeoides* (above & below)

Japanese hydrangea vine is an attractive, elegant vine that is related to climbing hydrangea, but it has a few interesting cultivars to add variety.

Growing

Japanese hydrangea vine grows well in **full sun** or **partial shade**. The soil should be **average to fertile, humus rich, moist** and **well drained**.

A smooth-surfaced wall is difficult for this vine to cling to, so attach a few supports to the wall and tie the plant to them. The dense growth will eventually hide the supports.

Tips

This vine will cling to any rough surface and looks attractive climbing a wall, fence, tree, pergola or arbor. It can also be used as a groundcover on a bank or allowed to grow up or over a rock wall.

Recommended

S. *hydrangeoides* is an attractive, climbing vine similar in appearance to climbing hydrangea. It bears lacy clusters of white flowers in mid-summer. '**Moonlight**' has silvery blue foliage. '**Roseum**' bears clusters of pink flowers.

This elegant vine adds a touch of glamour to even the most ordinary-looking home.

Features: clinging habit; dark green or silvery foliage; white or pink flowers **Height:** up to 40'
Spread: up to 40' **Hardiness:** zones 5–8

Passion Flower
Passiflora

P. incarnata

assion flower is a fast-growing, perennial climber that has unusual, intricate, colorful flowers. It is native to southern Missouri, and it may not be reliably perennial in a cold winter in the north. No worries, though, because it grows easily from seeds.

Growing
Grow passion flower in **full sun** or **partial shade**. This plant prefers **well-drained, moist** soil of **average fertility**. Keep it **sheltered** from wind and cold.

Tips
Passion flower is a popular addition to mixed containers and makes an unusual focal point near a door or other entryway. It works well along the edge of a woodland garden. The flowers attract hoards of butterflies.

The small, round to ovoid fruits are edible and can be eaten fresh or made into tasty preserves.

Recommended
P. incarnata is a fast growing, deciduous, perennial vine that climbs by use of tendrils. It has large, dark green leaves with three to five lobes. The fragrant, white to pinkish purple, bicolored flowers of summer are followed by edible, fleshy fruit that is yellow-green when ripe. **'Alba'** bears all-white flowers.

Fertilize passion flower sparingly. Too much nitrogen will encourage lots of foliage but few flowers.

Also called: Maypop **Features:** habit; foliage; exotic, white or pale pink flowers with blue or purple bands **Height:** 6–8' **Spread:** 3–6' **Hardiness:** zones (5) 6–9

Sweet Pea

Lathyrus

L. odoratus cultivars (above & below)

Sweet peas are among America's favorite climbing plants. Their fragrance is intoxicating.

You can help deter some diseases by not planting sweet peas in the same location two years in a row.

Growing

Sweet peas prefer **full sun** but tolerate light shade. The soil should be **fertile, high in organic matter, moist** and **well drained**. The plants tolerate light frost. Fertilize very lightly during the flowering season. Deadhead all spent blooms.

Soak the seeds in water for 24 hours or nick them with a nail file before planting. Plant them early, because sweet peas can stall and die off as the temperature rises. Provide mulch to keep the roots cool. Plant a second crop about a month after the first one for a longer blooming period.

Tips

Sweet peas grow up poles, trellises and fences or over rocks. They cling by wrapping tendrils around whatever they are growing up, so they do best when they have a rough surface, chain-link fence, small twigs or a net to cling to. The small, shrubby species and cultivars can be used in beds and borders.

Recommended

L. odoratus has many cultivars, in a range of sizes 1–6' tall and 6–12" wide, including some that are small and bushy rather than climbing. Heritage varieties are often the most fragrant. **'Bouquet Mix'** bears large flowers in a wide color range on long, heavy stems.

L. vernus (perennial sweet pea) is a compact, bushy perennial that grows 10–15" tall and wide. It bears violet-purple flowers that are often flushed red when young.

Features: clinging to bushy growth habit; pink, red, purple, lavender, blue, salmon, pale yellow, peach, white or bicolored summer flowers
Height: 10"–6' **Spread:** 6–15"
Hardiness: *L. odoratus* is a hardy annual; *L. vernus* is a perennial

Canna Lily

Canna

Canna lilies are stunning, dramatic plants that add an exotic flair to any garden.

Growing

Canna lilies grow best in **full sun,** in a **sheltered** location. The soil should be **fertile, moist** and **well drained**. Plant them out in spring, once the soil has warmed. Cannas can be started early indoors in containers to get a head start on the growing season. Deadhead to prolong blooming.

Tips

Canna lilies can be grown in a bed or border. They make dramatic specimen plants and can even be included in large planters.

Recommended

A wide range of canna lilies are available, including cultivars and hybrids with green, bronzy, purple or yellow-and-green-striped foliage. The flowers may be white, red, orange, pink, yellow or bicolored. Dwarf cultivars that grow 18–28" tall are also available.

C. hybrid (above & below)

Canna lily rhizomes can be lifted after the foliage is killed back in fall. Clean off any clinging dirt and store them in a cool, frost-free location in slightly moist peat moss. Check on them regularly through winter. If they begin to sprout, pot them and move them to a bright window until they can be moved outdoors.

Features: decorative foliage; white, red, orange, pink, yellow or bicolored summer flowers
Height: 18"–6' **Spread:** 20–36"
Hardiness: zones 7–8; grown as an annual

Crocus

Crocus

C. x *vernus* cultivars (above & below)

Crocuses are harbingers of spring. They often appear, as if by magic, in full bloom from beneath the melting snow.

Growing

Crocuses grow well in **full sun** or **light, dappled shade**. The soil should be of **poor to average fertility, gritty** and **well drained**. The corms are planted about 4" deep in fall.

Saffron is obtained from the dried, crushed stigmas of C. sativus. Typically, six plants produce enough spice for one recipe. This fall-blooming plant is hardy to zone 6 and is worth trying in southern Missouri.

Tips

Crocuses are almost always planted in groups. Drifts of crocuses can be planted in lawns to provide interest and color while the grass still lies dormant. In beds and borders, they can be left to naturalize. Groups of plants will fill in and spread out to provide a bright welcome in spring.

Recommended

Many crocus species, hybrids and cultivars are available. The spring-flowering crocus most people are familiar with is **C. x vernus**, commonly called Dutch crocus. Many cultivars are available, with flowers in shades of purple, yellow or white, sometimes bicolored or with darker veins. **'Pickwick'** has white flowers with violet purple stripes that can range from dark to pale. **'Purpureus Grandiflorus'** bears purple flowers in abundance.

Features: purple, yellow, white or bicolored flowers in early spring **Height:** 2–6" **Spread:** 2–4" **Hardiness:** zones 3–8

Daffodil

Narcissus

Many gardeners automatically think of large, trumpet-shaped, yellow flowers when they think of daffodils, but these bulbs offer a lot of variety in flower color, form and size.

Growing

Daffodils grow best in **full sun** or **light, dappled shade**. The soil should be **average to fertile, moist** and **well drained**. The bulbs should be planted in fall, 2–8" deep, depending on the size of the bulb. The bigger the bulb, the deeper it should be planted. As a guideline, measure the bulb from top to bottom and multiply that number by three to know how deeply to plant.

The cup in the center of a daffodil is called the corona, and the group of petals that surrounds the corona is called the perianth.

Tips

Daffodils are often planted where they can be left to naturalize, in the light shade beneath a tree or in a woodland garden. In mixed beds and borders, the faded leaves are hidden by the summer foliage of other plants.

Recommended

Many species, hybrids and cultivars of daffodils are available. The flowers come in shades of white, yellow, peach, orange or pink, or they may be bicolored. Solitary or borne in clusters, they range from 1½–6" across. There are 12 flower form categories.

Features: white, yellow, peach, orange, pink or bicolored spring flowers **Height:** 4–24" **Spread:** 4–12" **Hardiness:** zones 3–8

Flowering Onion
Allium

A. giganteum (above), A. cernuum (below)

Growing

Flowering onions grow best in **full sun**. The soil should be **average to fertile, moist** and **well drained**. Plant the bulbs in fall, 2–4" deep, depending on the bulb size.

Tips

Flowering onions are best planted in groups in a bed or border where they can be left to naturalize. Most self-seed when left to their own devices. The foliage, which tends to fade just as the plants come into flower, can be hidden with groundcover or a low, bushy companion plant.

Recommended

Several flowering onion species, hybrids and cultivars have gained popularity for their decorative pink, purple, white, yellow, blue or maroon flowers.

A. cernuum (nodding or wild onion) grows 12–24" tall and bears loose, drooping clusters of pink flowers in summer.

A. giganteum (giant onion) is a big plant up to 6' tall, with large, globe-shaped clusters of pinky purple flowers in summer.

A. moly (lily leek, golden garlic) grows 10–15" tall, with strap-like, gray-green to blue-green leaves and clusters of bright yellow flowers in late spring to early summer.

Flowering onions, with their striking, ball-like or loose, nodding clusters of flowers, are sure to attract attention.

Although the leaves of flowering onions have an onion scent when bruised, the flowers are often sweetly fragrant.

Features: pink, purple, white, yellow, blue or maroon flowers in late spring or summer; cylindrical or strap-shaped leaves **Height:** 10"–6' **Spread:** 2–12" **Hardiness:** zones 3–8

Hyacinth

Hyacinthus

The fragrance from one flower is powerful, but when hyacinth is planted en masse, the fragrance is absolutely intoxicating.

Growing

Hyacinth prefers **full sun** but tolerates partial shade. The soil should be **moist, well drained, moderately fertile** and **rich in organic matter**. Hyacinth prefers dry conditions when it is dormant in summer.

Plant the bulbs approximately 4–6" deep and 2–4" apart in fall, at least four to six weeks before the ground freezes. Ensure that the newly planted bulbs have adequate, but not excessive, water before the ground freezes.

Tips

Hyacinth looks great in beds, borders and containers, and it mixes very well with other spring-blooming bulbs. For a naturalistic effect, always plant the bulbs in odd numbers and groupings rather than in rows. Hyacinth bulbs are easy to force into bloom indoors.

Do not eat hyacinth because the plant parts are somewhat toxic. The sap may cause an allergic reaction in some people.

Recommended

H. orientalis has lance-shaped, bright green foliage and bears clusters of single or double flowers in many shades of purple, blue, white or pink. The vast array of hyacinth cultivars to choose from offers different sizes and flowering periods, including early-, mid- and late-spring bloom times.

Features: fragrant, colorful spring flowers in purple, blue, pink, white or cream; lengthy bloom time **Height:** 10–12" **Spread:** 4–6" **Hardiness:** zones 5–8

H. orientalis cultivar (above & below)

Hyacinth flowers are sensitive to hard spring frosts. In areas where these frosts are fairly common, plant hyacinth bulbs in a sheltered location and be ready to cover the tender plants if necessary.

Lily
Lilium

L. *Asiatic* Hybrids (above), L. 'Stargazer' (below)

Decorative clusters of large, richly colored blooms grace these tall plants. By choosing a variety of cultivars that flower at different times, it is possible to have lilies blooming all season.

Growing

Lilies grow best in **full sun,** but they like to have their roots shaded. The soil should be **rich in organic matter, fertile, moist** and **well drained**.

Tips

Lilies are often grouped in beds and borders and can be naturalized in woodland gardens and near water features. These plants are narrow but tall; plant at least three lilies together to create some volume.

Recommended

The many available species, hybrids and cultivars are grouped by type. Visit your local garden center to see what is available.

The following are two popular groups of lilies. **Asiatic hybrids** bear clusters of flowers in early summer or midsummer and are available in a wide range of colors. **Oriental hybrids** bear clusters of large, fragrant flowers in mid- and late summer. The usual colors are white, pink or red. **'Casa Blanca'** is an oriental hybrid that grows 3–4' tall and has large, bowl-shaped, fragrant, white flowers.

Lily bulbs should be planted in fall before the first frost, but they can also be planted in spring if bulbs are available.

Also called: oriental lily Features: early-, mid- or late-season flowers in shades of orange, yellow, peach, pink, purple, red or white Height: 2–5' Spread: 12" Hardiness: zones 4–8

Siberian Squill

Scilla

This easy-to-grow spring bloomer looks wonderful in mass plantings and is resistant to browsing by deer. Incredibly hardy and tolerant of adverse conditions, Siberian squill is often one of the first bulbs to bloom.

Growing

Siberian squill grows well in **full sun, partial shade** or **light shade,** in **average to fertile, humus rich, well-drained** soil. The bulbs should be planted 3–4" deep in fall, four to six weeks before the ground freezes. Plant them soon after purchase because they do not store well and may dry out.

Tips

Siberian squill makes a lovely addition to mixed beds and borders, where the bulbs can be interspersed amongst the other plants. They can also be planted into lawns, meadow gardens and woodland gardens, where they can be left to naturalize. Siberian squill is often most visually effective when planted en masse.

Recommended

S. siberica has wide, strap-shaped leaves and bears small clusters of nodding, bell-shaped, bright blue flowers in spring. Cultivars and varieties are available in different sizes and flower colors.

S. siberica (above & below)

Siberian squill can self-seed prolifically. Keep your eyes open for the small, grass-like seedlings so you can avoid pulling them up if you want more plants or remove them if you don't.

Features: dainty spring flowers in white, blue or purple; growth habit; tough as nails
Height: 3–8" **Spread:** 3–6"
Hardiness: zones 1–8

Snowdrop
Galanthus

G. elwesii (above), G. nivalis (below)

All parts of snowdrops are poisonous if ingested. Handling the bulbs may irritate sensitive skin.

When winter has you feeling dull and dreary, let early-blooming snowdrops bring some much-needed color to your winter garden.

Growing
Snowdrops grow well in **full sun** or **partial shade,** in **fertile, humus-rich, moist, well-drained** soil. Do not let the soil dry out in summer.

Tips
Snowdrops work well in beds, borders and rock gardens. For the best effect, snowdrops should always be planted in groups and close to each other. They can be planted in the lawn or under deciduous shrubs and trees that provide partial shade in summer. These flowers are great for naturalizing in lightly shaded woodlands.

Recommended
The various snowdrop species hybridize easily with each other; many hybrids are available.

G. elwesii (giant snowdrop) has larger flowers and foliage than *G. nivalis* and grows taller. The inner petals are heavily marked with green.

G. nivalis (common snowdrop) is a tiny plant that produces small, honey-scented, nodding, white flowers in mid- to late winter. The inner petals are marked with a green "V" shape. Cultivars are available, some with double flowers and some with yellow markings instead of green ones.

Features: early-blooming, white flowers; strap-like foliage; easy to grow **Height:** 4–12" **Spread:** 4–6" **Hardiness:** zones 3–8

Spanish Bluebells

Hyacinthoides

This genus of spring-blooming bulbs has experienced several name changes over the years, so don't be surprised to find it under a variety of botanical and common names. A great choice for Missouri gardens, Spanish bluebells are heat tolerant and prolific.

Growing

Spanish bluebells grow in full sun but perform best in **partial shade** or **deep shade**. The soil should be **rich, sandy** and very **well drained,** but Spanish bluebells tolerate a wide variety of soils as long as there is adequate moisture in spring.

Plant the bulbs soon after purchase because they do not store well and may dry out. The bulbs should be planted at least 3–4" deep and 3–6" apart from one another.

Tips

Spanish bluebells are most effective when planted in large groupings. They are ideal for areas that require a subtle touch of blue springtime color. These flowering bulbs can also be planted underneath deciduous shrubs for early spring interest. Naturalized areas also benefit from random plantings of Spanish bluebells, adding a hint of color in a meadow-like setting.

Recommended

H. hispanica *(Scilla campanulata; Scilla hispanica)* is a **Plant of Merit** that produces nodding, bell-shaped, blue flowers on 12–16" tall stems that rise through strap-like foliage. Cultivars with white or pink flowers are available.

H. hispanica culitvar (above), *H. hispanica* (below)

Also called: Spanish squill, wood hyacinth
Features: white, blue or pink spring flowers; habit; hardiness; tolerates poor conditions and shade **Height:** 12–16" **Spread:** 8–12"
Hardiness: zones 4–10

Summer Snowflake

Leucojum

L. aestivum (above), *L. aestivum* 'Gravetye Giant' (below)

Summer snowflake is one of the easiest bulbs to grow, with huge returns for little effort.

Growing

Summer snowflake grows well in areas with **full sun** or **partial shade,** and it tolerates areas that receive indirect bright light. The soil should be **moist** and **humus rich.** Do not let the soil dry out completely. *L. aestivum* tolerates constantly wet soil.

Tips

Flowering bulbs are always attractive in rock gardens. They can be used for naturalizing and planting in understories with adequate light. They also pack a punch when planted in large groups or en masse in mixed beds and borders.

Recommended

L. aestivum produces strap- or grass-like leaves in an upright clump. Nodding atop tall stems, the bell-shaped, white flowers are dotted with green at their tips and emit a chocolate-like scent. The species grows approximately 12–18" tall (with or without the flowers). **'Gravetye Giant'** grows taller than the species and produces larger flowers.

Summer snowflake has been shared with family and friends alike from one generation to the next.

Features: fragrant, nodding, white mid-spring flowers with green dots at petal tips; plant form **Height:** 12–18" **Spread:** 10–12" **Hardiness:** zones 4–9

Tulip

Tulipa

Tulips, with their beautiful, often garishly colored flowers, are a welcome sight as we enjoy the warm days of spring.

Growing

Tulips grow best in **full sun;** in light or partial shade, the flowers tend to bend toward the light. The soil should be **fertile** and **well drained**. Plant the bulbs in fall, 4–6" deep, depending on bulb size. Bulbs that have been cold treated can be planted in spring. Although tulips can repeat bloom, many hybrids perform best if planted new each year.

Tips

Tulips provide the best display when mass planted or planted in groups in flowerbeds and borders. They can also be grown in containers and can be forced to bloom early in pots indoors. Some of the species and old cultivars can be naturalized in meadow and wildflower gardens.

Recommended

There are about 100 species of tulips and thousands of hybrids and cultivars. They are generally divided into 15 groups based on bloom time and flower appearance. Dozens of colors are available, except blue, with many bicolored or multi-colored varieties. Shop in early fall for the best selection.

T. hybrids (above & below)

During the tulipomania of the 1630s, tulip bulbs were worth many times their weight in gold, and many tulip speculators lost massive fortunes when the mania subsided.

Features: spring flowers in any color except blue, or multi-colored   Height: 6–30"
Spread: 2–8"   Hardiness: zones 3–8; often treated as annuals

Winter Aconite

Eranthis

E. hyemalis (above & below)

One of the earliest plants to bloom, winter aconite produces a carpet of yellow flowers—a welcome sight that signals winter's end and the approach of spring.

Growing

Winter aconite grows well in **full sun** or **light shade**. The soil should be **fertile, humus rich, moist** and **well drained**. Plant the tubers about 3" deep. Winter aconite goes dormant during summer, but the soil should still be kept moist.

Tips

Winter aconite is a good plant for naturalizing in moist, lightly shaded areas under trees and shrubs. It can also be used around water features.

Recommended

E. hyemalis is a low, spreading plant. The whorls of leaves form a bright green ruff around the base of the yellow flowers. This plant grows 2–4" tall and can spread quickly and almost indefinitely to form large colonies.

The sap of winter aconite can cause skin irritation and, if ingested, stomach upset. Wear gloves, or wash your hands thoroughly after handling this plant.

Features: bright yellow flowers in early spring; glossy, green foliage
Height: 2–4" **Spread:** 24" to indefinite
Hardiness: zones 4–5

Basil

Ocimum

The sweet, fragrant leaves of fresh basil add a delicious flavor to salads and tomato-based dishes.

Growing

Basil grows best in a **warm, sheltered** location in **full sun**. The soil should be **fertile, moist** and **well drained**. Pinch the tips regularly to encourage bushy growth. Plant seedlings out or direct sow the seed after frost danger has passed in spring.

Tips

Although basil grows best in a warm spot outdoors, it can be grown successfully in a pot by a bright window indoors to provide you with fresh leaves all year.

Recommended

O. basilicum is one of the most popular of the culinary herbs. The dozens of varieties include ones with large or tiny, green or purple and smooth or ruffled leaves.

O. basilicum 'Genovese' and 'Cinnamon' (above)
O. basilicum 'Genovese' (below)

Basil is a good companion plant for tomatoes—both like warm, moist growing conditions, and, when you pick tomatoes for a salad, you'll also remember to include a few sprigs or leaves of basil.

Features: fragrant, decorative leaves
Height: 12–24" **Spread:** 12–18"
Hardiness: tender annual

Chives

Allium

A. schoenoprasum (above & below)

The delicate onion flavor of chives is best enjoyed fresh. Mix chives into dips or sprinkle them on salads and baked potatoes.

Growing

Chives grow best in **full sun**. The soil should be **fertile, moist** and **well drained,** but chives adapt to most soil conditions. These plants are easy to start from seed, but they do like the soil temperature to stay above 66° F before they germinate, so seeds started directly in the garden are unlikely to sprout before early summer.

Tips

Chives are decorative enough to be included in a mixed or herbaceous border and can be left to naturalize. In an herb garden, chives should be given plenty of space to allow self-seeding.

Recommended

A. **schoenoprasum** forms a clump of cylindrical, bright green leaves. Clusters of pinky purple flowers are produced in early and mid-summer. Varieties with white or pink flowers are available.

Chives spread with reckless abandon as the clumps grow larger and the plants self-seed.

Chives are said to increase appetite and encourage good digestion.

Features: foliage; form; purple, white or pink flowers **Height:** 8–24" **Spread:** 12" or more **Hardiness:** zones 3–8

Dill

Anethum

Dill leaves and seeds are probably best known for their use as pickling herbs, although they have a wide variety of other culinary uses.

Growing

Dill grows best in **full sun,** in a **sheltered location** out of strong winds. The soil should be of **poor to average fertility, moist** and **well drained**. To ensure a regular supply of leaves, sow seeds every few weeks in spring and early summer. These plants should not be grown near fennel because the two species cross-pollinate, causing the seeds to lose their distinct flavors.

Tips

With its feathery leaves, dill is an attractive addition to a mixed bed or border. It can be included in a vegetable garden, but it does well in any sunny location. It also attracts beneficial predatory insects to the garden.

Recommended

A. graveolens forms a clump of feathery foliage. Clusters of yellow flowers are borne at the tops of sturdy stems.

A. graveolens (above & below)

Dill turns up frequently in historical records as both a culinary and medicinal herb. It was used by the ancient Egyptians and Romans, and it is mentioned in the Bible.

Features: feathery, edible foliage; yellow summer flowers; edible seeds
Height: 2–5' **Spread:** 12" or more
Hardiness: annual

Lavender

Lavandula

L. angustifolia (above & below)

Heavenly aromatic flowers and silvery gray-green foliage make lavender a great accent for mixed plantings or as an anchor in the herb garden.

Growing

Lavender grows best in **full sun**. The soil should be **average to fertile** and **alkaline,** and it *must* be **well drained**. Established plants tolerate heat and drought. Protect it from winter cold and wind. In cold areas, lavender should be covered with mulch and, if possible, a good layer of snow.

Trim lavender back in late summer and spring to keep it from becoming too woody. Never cut into old growth. New buds emerging in spring show you how far back you can cut—leave at least one of the new buds. Avoid heavy pruning after August to give it time to harden off before winter.

Tips

Lavender is a wonderful, aromatic edging plant and can be used to form a low hedge. To dry the flowers, cut them when they show full color but before they open completely.

Recommended

L. angustifolia (English lavender) is an aromatic, bushy subshrub that is often treated as a perennial. From mid-summer to fall, it bears spikes of small flowers. Cultivars of varying size are available. **'Hidcote'** and **'Munstead'** are the most reliably hardy cultivars for northern areas of the state.

Features: purple, pink, blue or red flowers from mid-summer to fall; fragrance; foliage; habit **Height:** 8–36" **Spread:** 2–4'
Hardiness: zones 5–9

Oregano • Marjoram

Origanum

Oregano and marjoram are two of the best known and most frequently used herbs. They are popular in stuffings, soups and stews, and no pizza is complete until it has been sprinkled with fresh or dried oregano leaves.

Growing

Oregano and marjoram grow best in **full sun**. The soil should be of **poor to average fertility, neutral to alkaline** and **well drained**. The flowers attract pollinators to the garden.

Tips

These bushy perennials make a lovely addition to any border and can be trimmed to form low hedges.

Recommended

O. majorana (marjoram) is upright and shrubby, with hairy, light green leaves. It bears white or pink flowers in summer and can be grown as an annual where it is not hardy.

O. vulgare var. *hirtum* (oregano, Greek oregano) is the most flavorful culinary variety of oregano. The low, bushy plant has hairy, gray-green leaves and bears white flowers. Many other interesting varieties of *O. vulgare* are available, including ones with golden, variegated or curly leaves.

O. vulgare 'Aureum' (above & below)

In Greek, oros means "mountain," and ganos means "joy" or "beauty," so oregano translates as "joy (or beauty) of the mountain."

Features: fragrant foliage; white or pink summer flowers; bushy habit **Height:** 12–32"
Spread: 8–18" **Hardiness:** zones 5–8

Parsley
Petroselinum

P. crispum (above), *P. crispum* var. *crispum* (below)

Although usually used as a garnish, parsley is rich in vitamins and minerals and is reputed to freshen the breath after garlic or onion-rich foods are eaten.

Growing

Parsley grows well in **full sun** or **partial shade**. The soil should be of **average to rich fertility, humus rich, moist** and **well drained**. Direct sow the seeds because the plants resent transplanting. If you start seeds early, use peat pots so the plants can be potted or planted out without disruption.

Tips

Parsley should be started where you mean to grow it.

Containers of parsley can be kept close to the house for easy picking. The bright green leaves and compact growth habit make parsley a good edging plant for beds and borders.

Recommended

P. crispum forms a clump of divided, bright green leaves. This biennial is usually grown as an annual. Cultivars may have flat or curly leaves. Flat leaves are more flavorful, and curly are more decorative. Dwarf cultivars are also available. **Var.** *neopolitanum* (Italian parsley) has flat, dark green leaves with a particularly strong flavor.

Parsley leaves make a tasty and nutritious addition to salads. Tear freshly picked leaves and sprinkle them over your mixed greens or mix them in.

Features: attractive foliage **Height:** 8–24"
Spread: 12–24" **Hardiness:** zones 5–8;
grown as an annual

Rosemary

Rosmarinus

*T*he needle-like leaves of rosemary are used to flavor a wide variety of culinary dishes, including chicken, pork, lamb, rice, tomato and egg dishes.

Growing

Rosemary prefers **full sun,** but it tolerates partial shade. The soil should be of **poor to average fertility** and **well drained**.

Tips

Where it is hardy, rosemary is often grown in a shrub border. In Missouri, it is often grown in a container as a specimen or with other plants. Low-growing, spreading plants can be included in a rock garden or along the top of a retaining wall, or they can be grown in hanging baskets.

Recommended

R. officinalis is a dense, bushy, evergreen shrub with narrow, dark green leaves. The habit varies somewhat between cultivars, from strongly upright to prostrate and spreading. The flowers are usually in shades of blue, but pink-flowered cultivars are available. Cultivars are available that can survive in zone 6 in a sheltered location with winter protection. Plants rarely reach their mature size when grown in containers.

To overwinter a container-grown rosemary, keep it in very light or partial shade in summer, then put it in a sunny window indoors for winter and keep it well watered but not soaking wet.

R. officinalis (above & below)

Features: fragrant, evergreen foliage; bright blue, sometimes pink, summer flowers
Height: 8"–4' **Spread:** 1–4'
Hardiness: zone 8

Sage
Salvia

S. *officinalis* 'Icterina' (above)
S. *officinalis* 'Purpurea' (below)

Sage has been used since at least ancient Greek times as a medicinal and culinary herb and continues to be widely used for both those purposes today.

Sage is perhaps best known as a flavoring for stuffing, but it has a great range of uses, including adding it to soups, stews, sausages and dumplings.

Growing
Sage prefers **full sun** but tolerates light shade. The soil should be of **average fertility** and **well drained**. This plant benefits from a light mulch of compost each year. It tolerates drought once established.

Tips
Sage is an attractive plant for the border, adding volume to the middle or as an attractive edging or feature plant near the front. Sage can also be grown in mixed planters.

Recommended
S. *officinalis* is a woody, mounding plant with soft, gray-green leaves. Spikes of light purple flowers appear in early and mid-summer. Many cultivars with attractive foliage are available, including the silver-leaved **'Berggarten,'** the yellow-margined **'Icterina,'** the purple-leaved **'Purpurascens'** and the variegated, purple-green and cream **'Tricolor,'** which has a pink flush to the new growth.

Features: fragrant, decorative foliage; blue or purple summer flowers **Height:** 12–24"
Spread: 18–36" **Hardiness:** zones 5–8

Tarragon
Artemisia

The distinctive licorice flavor of tarragon lends itself to a wide variety of meat and vegetable dishes and is the key flavoring in Bernaise sauce.

Growing
Tarragon grows best in **full sun**. The soil should be **average to fertile, moist** and **well drained**. Divide the plants every few years to keep them growing vigorously and to encourage the best leaf flavor.

Tips
These plants are not exceptionally decorative and can be included in an herb garden or mixed border where their tall stems will be supported by the surrounding plants.

Recommended
A. dracunculus var. *sativa* (French or German tarragon) is a bushy plant with tall stems and narrow leaves. Airy clusters of insignificant flowers are produced in late summer.

A. dracunculus var. sativa (above & below)

Two types of tarragon are available. French tarragon is the preferred culinary selection, whereas Russian tarragon is a weedy plant that is grown from seed but has little of the desired flavor. French tarragon is grown from cuttings. Chew a leaf from the plant; if you don't notice the distinctive licorice flavor, don't buy it.

Features: flavorful foliage **Height:** 18–36"
Spread: 12–18" **Hardiness:** zones 3–8

Thyme
Thymus

T. vulgaris (above), T. x citrodorus (below)

Thymes are bee magnets when in bloom; thyme honey is pleasantly herbal and goes very well with biscuits.

Thymes are popular culinary herbs used in soups, stews and casseroles and with roasts.

Growing
Thymes prefer **full sun**. The soil should be **neutral to alkaline** and of **poor to average fertility**. **Good drainage** is essential. It is beneficial to work leaf mould and sharp limestone gravel into the soil to improve structure and drainage.

Tips
Thymes are useful for sunny, dry locations at the front of borders, between or beside paving stones, on rock gardens and rock walls or in containers.

Once the plants have finished flowering, shear them back by about half to encourage new growth and to prevent them from becoming too woody.

Recommended
T. **x** *citriodorus* (lemon-scented thyme) forms a mound of lemon-scented, dark green foliage. The flowers are pale pink. Cultivars with silver- or gold-margined leaves are available.

T. vulgaris (common thyme) forms a bushy mound of dark green leaves. The flowers may be purple, pink or white. Cultivars with variegated leaves are available.

Features: bushy habit; fragrant, decorative foliage; purple, pink or white flowers
Height: 8–16" **Spread:** 8–16"
Hardiness: zones 4–8

Ajuga
Ajuga

A. *reptans* CHOCOLATE CHIP (above), A. *reptans* 'Caitlin's Giant' (below)

Often considered to be a rampant runner, ajuga grows best where it can roam freely without competition.

Growing

Ajuga develops the best leaf color in **partial** or **light shade** but tolerates full shade; too much sun may scorch the leaves. Any **well-drained** soil is suitable. Divide this vigorous plant any time during the growing season. Remove any new growth or seedlings that don't show the hybrid leaf coloring.

Tips

Ajuga makes an excellent groundcover for difficult sites, such as exposed slopes and dense shade. It also looks attractive in shrub borders, where its dense growth prevents the spread of all but the most tenacious weeds.

Recommended

A. reptans is a low, quick-spreading groundcover. Many cultivars with colorful, often variegated foliage are available. **'Burgundy Glow'** has variegated foliage in shades of bronze, green, white and pink. The habit is dense and compact. **'Caitlin's Giant'** has large, bronze leaves and bears short spikes of bright blue flowers. CHOCOLATE CHIP (*A.* x *tenorii* 'Valfredda') is a low, creeping plant with teardrop-shaped, chocolate-bronze leaves and spikes of blue flowers.

Ajuga combines well with hostas and ferns, and it enjoys the same shady sites and growing conditions.

Also called: bugleweed
Features: colorful, decorative foliage; late-spring to early-summer flowers in purple, blue, pink or white **Height:** 3–12"
Spread: 6–12" **Hardiness:** zones 3–8

Bishop's Hat
Epimedium

E. x youngianum 'Niveum' (above), *E. x rubrum* (below)

Plant Bishop's hat in a location where the beautiful foliage and flowers are easily seen, especially in fall.

Growing

Bishop's hat prefers **partial shade** and **rich, moist, well-drained** soil. Protect it from cold, dry winds. Most varieties tolerate drought. Mulch in mid- to late fall to provide winter protection and maintain adequate soil moisture. Divide in fall.

Shear back the oldest foliage and flowers in late winter or early spring, before the new flower buds emerge.

Tips

Bishop's hat is best used as a groundcover in shady locations, in a woodland setting or on the side of a sheltered wall.

Recommended

E. x rubrum (red barrenwort) is a spreading, clump-forming plant with pink and yellow bicolored flowers. The reddish green foliage tinge intensifies with age.

E. x versicolor forms mounds of finely divided foliage. Young foliage is coppery red, fading to green with age. The small flowers are a deep reddish pink with yellow petals. '**Sulphureum**' is a **Plant of Merit** that bears yellow flowers with long spurs.

E. x youngianum has green foliage and red-tinted stems. It bears white or pale pink flowers, sometimes with spurs. '**Niveum**' bears white flowers.

Also called: barrenwort **Features:** spring and summer flowers in red, pink, purple, white or yellow; attractive foliage **Height:** 8–12" **Spread:** 8–12" **Hardiness:** zones 4–8

Blue Fescue
Festuca

F. glauca 'Elijah Blue' (above), *F. glauca* (below)

Blue fescue was one of the first ornamental grasses to appear on the market over a decade ago. Blue fescue continues to display its finest features in harsh conditions.

Growing
Fescue prefers **full sun** and **poor to moderately fertile, well-drained** soil. Keep the soil a little on the dry side.

Tips
The low-growing tufts of blue fescue are used as edging for beds and borders, and they look great when mass planted. It is frequently used in xeriscape settings and naturalized areas. The low-growing fescues also work well in rock and alpine gardens.

Recommended
F. glauca (*F. ovina* var. *glauca;* blue sheep's fescue) produces steely blue tufts of fine, needle-like blades of grass. Most varieties produce tan-colored flower spikes that rise above the mounds of blue foliage. A great many cultivars and hybrids are available. **'Elijah Blue'** has soft, powdery blue foliage.

Fescue specimens can be divided every two to three years or when they begin to die out in the centers. Division helps to maintain the foliage color.

Features: colorful foliage; flower spikes; growth habit **Height:** 6–18"
Spread: 10–12" **Hardiness:** zones 3–8

Blue Oat Grass

Helictotrichon

H. sempervirens (above & below)

Blue oat grass is easily propagated by division in early spring. Reliable in Missouri, it is a cool-season perennial.

This hardy grass is the perfect plant for people who desire a super-sized version of blue fescue for their gardens.

Growing

Blue oat grass thrives in **full sun**. The soil should be **average to dry** and **well drained**. This grass is considered to be evergreen, but it still needs a trim in spring to encourage new growth and simply to tidy it up.

Tips

This large, nonspreading grass is ideal for just about any setting, from beds and borders to containers. It works well in a xeriscape design or naturalized area. Its wonderful color, impressive size and growth habit make it a lovely complement to flowering perennials and shrubs.

Recommended

H. sempervirens is a large, coarse-textured grass that produces perfectly rounded, dome-shaped clumps of intensely blue foliage. Wiry, tan stems tipped with tan seedheads emerge through the foliage.

Features: brilliant blue foliage; decorative spikes of tan seedheads **Height:** 2–4'
Spread: 24–30" **Hardiness:** zones 3–8

Christmas Fern

Polystichum

P. acrostichoides (above & below)

Christmas fern is one of the lower-growing and less invasive of the hardy ferns. It is native to a large swath of eastern North America, from Canada to Florida and inland from Minnesota to Texas.

Growing

Christmas fern grows well in **partial to full shade**. The soil should be **fertile, humus rich** and **moist**.

Divide this fern in spring to propagate it or to control its spread. In spring, before the new fronds fill in, remove the ones that are dead or look worn out.

Tips

Christmas fern can be used in beds and borders, and it is a good choice for a shaded pondside garden. It is better suited to moist rather than wet conditions.

The use of the fronds as Christmas decorations gave the plant its common name. Christmas fern is mostly deer proof.

Recommended

P. acrostichoides is a vase-shaped, evergreen, perennial fern that forms a circular clump of arching, lance-shaped, dark green fronds. The fertile fronds are shorter and slightly wider than the sterile fronds. This wonderful Missouri native fern is a **Plant of Merit** selection.

Features: evergreen foliage; easy to grow; problem free **Height:** 12–18"
Spread: 18–36" **Hardiness:** zones 3–9

Dead Nettle
Lamium

L. maculatum 'White Nancy' (above), *L. maculatum* 'Beacon Silver' (below)

These attractive plants hug the ground and thrive on only the barest necessities of life.

Growing

Dead nettles prefer **partial shade** or **light shade** and **humus-rich, moist, well-drained** soil of **average fertility**. Growth is very vigorous in fertile soil. These plants can develop bare patches if the soil is allowed to dry out for extended periods. If bare spots become unsightly, divide and replant in fall.

If your dead nettles become invasive and overwhelm other plants, simply pull some of them up, making sure to remove the fleshy roots.

Tips

Dead nettles plants make useful groundcovers for woodland or shade gardens. They work well under shrubs in a border, where they help keep weeds down.

When sheared back after flowering, dead nettles remain compact. If they remain green over winter, shear them back in early spring.

Recommended

L. galeobdolon (*Lamiastrum galeobdolon;* yellow archangel) has yellow flowers and can be quite invasive, although the cultivars are less so.

L. maculatum (spotted dead nettle) is a low-growing, spreading species. The green leaves are marked with varying degrees of white or silver, and the flowers are white, pink or mauve. The following cultivars have silver foliage with green margins. **'Beacon Silver'** has pink flowers. **'Orchid Frost'** has deep pink flowers. **'White Nancy'** has white flowers.

Features: decorative, often variegated foliage; white, pink, yellow or mauve flowers in spring or summer **Height:** 4–24"
Spread: indefinite **Hardiness:** zones 3–8

Dusty Miller
Senecio

S. cineraria 'Cirrus' (above), *S. cineraria* (below)

We often look only at a plant's flowers when choosing what to include in our gardens. Do not underestimate the value of a plant's foliage. Dusty miller is an excellent plant for providing contrast in beds or containers of colorful flowers and green foliage.

Growing
Dusty miller prefers **full sun** but tolerates light shade. The soil should be of **average fertility** and **well drained**.

Tips
The soft, lacy, silvery leaves of this plant are its main feature. Dusty miller is used primarily as an edging plant, but it is also effective in beds, borders and containers. The silvery foliage makes a good backdrop to show off the brightly colored flowers of other plants.

Some gardeners pinch off the yellow to white flowers before they bloom. They aren't that showy, and they use energy that would otherwise go to producing more foliage.

Recommended
S. cineraria forms a mound of lobed or finely divided, fuzzy, silvery gray foliage. Many cultivars with impressive foliage colors and shapes have been developed.

Mix dusty miller with geraniums, begonias or cockscombs to bring out the vibrant colors of those flowers.

Features: silvery foliage; neat habit; easy to grow **Height:** 12–24" **Spread:** equal to height or slightly less **Hardiness:** tender perennial treated as an annual

Flowering Fern
Osmunda

O. regalis (above), O. cinnamomea (below)

A flowering fern's "flowers" are actually its spore-producing sporangia.

*F*erns have a certain prehistoric mystique, and they can add a graceful elegance and textural accent to the garden.

Growing
Flowering ferns prefer **light shade** but tolerate full sun in consistently moist soil. The soil should be **fertile, humus rich, acidic** and **moist,** although wet soil is tolerated. Flowering ferns spread by offsets that form at the plant bases.

Tips
These large ferns form an attractive mass when planted in large colonies. They can be included in beds and borders, and they make a welcome addition to a woodland garden.

Recommended
O. cinnamomea (cinnamon fern) has light green fronds that fan out in a circular fashion from a central point. Leafless, bright green, fertile fronds that mature to cinnamon brown are produced in spring and stand straight up in the center of the plant.

O. regalis (royal fern) forms a dense clump of foliage. Feathery, flower-like, fertile fronds stand out among the sterile fronds in summer; they mature to a rusty brown. **'Purpurescens'** has fronds that contrast well with the purple stems; they are purple-red when they emerge in spring and mature to green. (Zones 3–8)

Features: perennial, deciduous fern; decorative, fertile fronds; habit **Height:** 30"–5' **Spread:** 24–36" **Hardiness:** zones 2–8

Fountain Grass

Pennisetum

*T*he low maintenance requirements and graceful form of fountain grasses make them easy to place. They soften any landscape, even in winter.

Growing

Fountain grasses thrive in **full sun,** in **well-drained** soil of **average fertility,** and established plants tolerate drought. These plants may self-seed, but they are not troublesome. Shear perennial selections back in early spring and divide them when they start to die out in the center.

Tips

Fountain grasses can be used as individual specimen plants, in group plantings and drifts or combined with flowering annuals, perennials, shrubs or other ornamental grasses. Annual selections are often planted in containers.

Recommended

P. alopecuroides '**Hameln**' (dwarf perennial fountain grass) is a compact cultivar with silvery white plumes and narrow, dark green leaves that turn gold in fall.

P. setaceum (annual fountain grass) has narrow, green leaves and pinkish purple flowers that mature to gray. '**Rubrum**' (red annual fountain grass) has broader, deep burgundy leaves and pinkish purple flowers.

P. glaucum '**Purple Majesty**' (purple ornamental millet) has blackish purple foliage and coarse, bottlebrush flowers. This annual's form resembles a corn stalk.

Features: arching, fountain-like habit; colorful foliage; flowers; winter interest
Height: 2–5' **Spread:** 24–36"
Hardiness: zones 5–8 or annual

P. glaucum 'Purple Majesty' (above)
P. setaceum 'Rubrum' (below)

Inland Sea Oats
Chasmanthium

C. latifolium (above & below)

The flower stalks of inland sea oats, which resemble strings of dangling fish, make interesting additions to fresh or dried arrangements.

This Missouri native grass is at home in moist, shady woodlands, and its bamboo-like foliage gives it a tropical flair.

Growing

Inland sea oats thrives in **full sun** (must stay moist to avoid leaf scorch) or **partial shade;** the upright, cascading habit relaxes in deep shade. The soil should be **fertile** and **moist,** but dry soils are tolerated. To deal with the vigorous self-seeding, deadhead in fall or pull the easily removed seedlings for sharing with friends or composting. Cut this plant back each spring to 2" above the ground. Divide it to control its rapid spread.

Tips

Inland sea oats is a tremendous plant for moist, shady areas. Its upright to cascading habit, especially when in full bloom, is attractive alongside a stream or pond, in a large drift or in a container.

Recommended

C. latifolium forms a spreading clump of bamboo-like, bright green foliage. The scaly, dangling spikelet flowers arrange themselves nicely on delicate stems, just slightly above the foliage. The foliage sometimes turns bronze, and the flowers turn gold in fall.

Also called: Indian wood oats, spangle grass
Features: bamboo-like foliage; unusual flowers; winter interest **Height:** 32"–4'
Spread: 18–24" **Hardiness:** zones 5–8

Maidenhair Fern

Adiantum

A. pedatum (above & below)

This charming and delicate-looking native fern adds a graceful touch to any woodland planting. Its unique habit and texture stand out in any garden.

Growing

Maidenhair fern grows well in **light shade** or **partial shade** and tolerates full shade. The soil should be of **average fertility, humus rich, slightly acidic** and **moist**. This plant rarely needs dividing, but it can be divided in spring to propagate more plants.

Tips

Maidenhair fern does well in any shaded spot in the garden. Include it in rock gardens, woodland gardens, shaded borders or beneath shade trees. It also makes an attractive addition to a shaded planting next to a water feature or on a slope where the foliage can be seen when it sways in the breeze.

Also called: northern maidenhair fern
Features: summer and fall foliage; habit
Height: 12–24" **Spread:** 12–24"
Hardiness: zones 2–8

Recommended

A. pedatum is a deciduous perennial fern that forms a spreading mound of delicate, arching fronds. Light green leaflets stand out against the black stems, and the whole plant turns bright yellow in fall. Spores are produced on the undersides of the leaflets.

To create a nice contrast in texture, try growing the fine-textured and delicate maidenhair fern with hostas, lungwort (Pulmonaria) *and brunnera.*

Mazus
Mazus

M. reptans (left & right)

Mazus is a tough, easy-to-grow groundcover that can handle being walked on and will not run rampant over neighboring plants. It is a great cover for spring-blooming bulbs.

Growing

Mazus grows well in **full sun, partial shade** or **light shade**. The soil should be of **average fertility, moist** and **well drained**. Mazus does best with some **shelter** from drying winds, and the plant suffers if the soil is allowed to dry out. It is easily divided or grown from seed. Sow the seeds in containers in a cold frame in spring or fall.

Tips

Mazus is great as a groundcover. It looks wonderful in rock gardens and in the cracks and spaces between patio stones. It can handle foot traffic.

Recommended

M. reptans is a **Plant of Merit**. It is a semi-evergreen, tufted perennial that forms a dense, low mat of creeping stems that root where the nodes touch the ground. The diminutive leaves are medium green and coarsely toothed, and they can turn bronzy red in fall. In late spring to early summer, this plant bears clusters of purple-blue flowers, their lower lips dotted with white, yellow and red spots.

Take care where you plant this attractive groundcover. Mazus can invade lawns, so make sure to keep it trimmed back from those areas.

Also called: creeping mazus **Features:** colorful flowers; spreading habit **Height:** 1–2" **Spread:** 8–12" for individual plants **Hardiness:** zones 5–8

Miscanthus

Miscanthus

Miscanthus is one of the most popular and majestic of all the ornamental grasses. Its graceful foliage dances in the wind and makes an impressive sight all year long.

Growing

Miscanthus prefers **full sun**. The soil should be of **average fertility, moist** and **well drained,** although some selections also tolerate wet soil. All selections tolerate drought once established.

Tips

Give these magnificent beauties room to spread so you can fully appreciate their form. The plant's height determines the best place for each selection in the border. They create dramatic impact in groups or as seasonal screens.

Recommended

There are many available cultivars of **M. sinensis,** all distinguished by the white midrib on the leaf blade. **'Adagio'** is one of the smallest cultivars. This **Plant of Merit** forms a compact clump of silvery gray-green foliage that turns yellow to bronze in fall. The pinkish plumes fade to creamy white when mature. **'Gracillimus'** (maiden grass) has long, fine-textured leaves and reddish plumes. **'Morning Light'** (variegated maiden grass) is a delicate plant that has very narrow, green leaves with

M. sinensis 'Strictus' (above)
M. sinensis 'Zebrinus' (below)

fine white edges and pinkish plumes. **'Strictus'** (porcupine grass) is a tall, stiff, upright selection with unusual horizontal, yellow bands. **'Zebrinus'** (zebra grass) has arching foliage and yellow, horizontal bands.

Also called: eulalia, Japanese silver grass
Features: upright, arching habit; colorful summer and fall foliage; pink, copper or silver flowers in late summer and fall; winter interest
Height: 2–8' **Spread:** 2–4'
Hardiness: zones 5–8; possibly zone 4

Mondo Grass
Ophiopogon

O. planiscapus 'Nigrescens' (above & below)

Easy to grow and dependable, mondo gras s is dense enough to out-compete weeds. It requires very minimal maintenance.

Growing

Mondo grass prefers to grow in **full sun to light shade**, in **moist, moderately fertile, well-drained, humus-rich** soil. The foliage is at its best in full sun. Divide in spring, just as new growth resumes. This plant appreciates a layer of thick mulch for winter protection and may not survive a cold winter in the northern part of our state.

Mondo grass is a member of the lily family and does not like being mowed.

Tips

Mondo grass can be used as a dense groundcover, as it spreads slowly by rhizomes. Use it for border edges or in containers. In cool zones, it can be dug up and stored for winter in a cool, dark room.

Recommended

O. planiscapus (black mondo grass, black lily turf) **'Ebknizam'** (EBONY NIGHT) has curving, almost black leaves and dark lavender flowers. It grows 4–6" tall and 6–12" wide. **'Nigrescens'** is an **Emeritus Plant of Merit** that has curving, almost black foliage and pink, often white-flushed flowers. It grows 6–12" tall and 12" wide. Both cultivars produce blackish, berry-like fruit.

Features: uniquely colored foliage; groundcover habit; lavender or pink, often white-flushed flowers **Height:** 4–12" **Spread:** 6–12" **Hardiness:** zones (5) 6–9

Muhlygrass
Muhlenbergia

Muhlygrass is a tough-as-nails grass that tolerates drought, floods, salt, heat and humidity. It is at home in a wild, native garden or in a formal border.

Growing

Muhlygrass thrives in **full sun** and tolerates light shade. The soil should be **well drained, slightly acidic** and **moist,** although it tolerates just about any type of soil. Established plants prefer infrequent watering, but more water results in larger plants.

For thicker clumps, leave the ripened seedheads in place to allow self-seeding; otherwise, remove the seedheads before they ripen and fall. Muhlygrass can be cut back in spring, just as the new growth begins, but this plant can be equally stunning when the new growth emerges through the previous year's growth.

Tips

This wild-looking, medium-sized grass is suited to mixed beds and borders. It looks great with coarse-textured plants that bring attention to its delicate form. It's also useful for naturalizing areas of your garden that require little attention or care, and it works well as a groundcover in areas with poor soil. The fall color stands out at a time when most other plants look spent.

Recommended

M. capillaris produces a dense, showy, knee-high clump of fine, wispy, grayish green grass. Purplish to pinkish flowerheads begin to emerge in late summer and last for up to two months.

M. capillaris (above & below)

Also called: mist grass, hairy awn muhly, pink muhlygrass, purple muhlygrass, pink hair grass **Features:** attractive form; pink to purple seedheads in fall **Height:** 24–36" **Spread:** 24–36" **Hardiness:** zones 5–10

Ostrich Fern

Matteuccia

M. struthiopteris (above & below)

This popular, classic fern is revered for its delicious emerging spring fronds and its stately, vase-shaped habit.

Growing

Ostrich fern prefers **partial or light shade** but tolerates full shade and even full sun if the soil is kept moist. The soil should be **average to fertile, humus rich, neutral to acidic** and **moist;** the leaves may scorch if the soil is not moist enough.

This fern reproduces by spores. Unwanted plants can be pulled up and composted or given away.

Tips

Ostrich fern appreciates a moist woodland garden and is often found growing wild alongside woodland streams and creeks. Useful in shaded borders, it is quick to spread, to the delight of anyone who enjoys the young fronds as a culinary delicacy.

Ostrich fern is also grown commercially for its edible fiddleheads. The tightly coiled, new spring fronds taste delicious when lightly steamed and served with butter. Remove the bitter, papery, reddish brown coating before steaming.

Recommended

M. struthiopteris (*M. pennsylvanica*) is a hardy perennial fern that forms a circular cluster of slightly arching, feathery fronds. Stiff, brown, fertile fronds, covered in reproductive spores, stick up in the center of the cluster in late summer and persist through winter. They are popular choices for dried arrangements.

Also called: fiddlehead fern **Features:** foliage; habit **Height:** 3–5' **Spread:** 12–36" or more **Hardiness:** zones 1–8

Prairie Dropseed

Sporobolus

S. *heterolepis* (left & right)

Prairie dropseed boasts graceful fountains of attractive summer and fall foliage; its flowers are fragrant and showy, and it is often visible above the snow during winter.

Growing

Prairie dropseed grows best in **full sun,** in **rocky, well-drained** soil. It is extremely tolerant of heat and drought, but it appreciates occasional moisture. It tolerates a range of soils, including heavy clay. Prairie dropseed can self-seed, but it is not a rampant spreader.

Sow the seeds in spring or fall where they are to grow. Divide prairie dropseed in spring or fall to propagate more plants.

Also called: rushgrass **Features:** summer and fall foliage; fragrant, airy flowers; low maintenance **Height:** 18–40"
Spread: 24" **Hardiness:** zones 3–9

Tips

A Missouri native, prairie dropseed is at home in meadows and native plantings. This versatile grass can be used for texture and color accents in beds, borders, containers or rock gardens. It is effective for erosion control, and it makes a great groundcover for hot, dry areas. The flowering stems make great additions to dried flower arrangements.

Recommended

*S. **heterolepis*** is a slow-growing, long-lived, clump-forming, perennial grass that has arching, very narrow, emerald green foliage that turns golden yellow with orange highlights in fall. It is a **Plant of Merit**. Cloud-like clusters of pendant, fragrant, pale pink flowers are borne above the mound of foliage in late summer.

Reed Grass
Calamagrostis

C. x acutiflora 'Overdam' (above)
C. x acutiflora 'Karl Foerster' (below)

This graceful grass changes its habit and flower color throughout the growing season. The slightest breeze keeps it in perpetual motion.

Growing
Reed grass grows best in **full sun**. The ideal soil is **fertile, moist** and **well drained**, although heavy clay and dry soils are tolerated. Grow this plant in areas with good air circulation. Rain and heavy snow may cause it to flop, but it quickly bounces back. Cut back to 2–4" in very early spring, before growth begins. Divide reed grass if it begins to die out in the center.

Tips
Whether it's used as a single, stately focal point, in small groupings or in large drifts, this plant is a desirable, low-maintenance grass. It combines well with perennials that bloom in late summer and fall.

Recommended
C. x *acutiflora* 'Karl Foerster' (Foerster's feather reed grass) is a **Plant of Merit** that forms a loose mound of green foliage from which the airy bottle-brush flowers emerge in June. The flowering stems have a loose, arching habit when they first emerge, but they grow more stiff and upright over summer. Other cultivars include 'Avalanche,' which has a white center stripe, and 'Overdam,' a compact, less hardy selection with white leaf edges.

Also called: feather reed grass
Features: open habit, becoming upright; silvery pink flowers that turn rich tan; green foliage that turns bright gold in fall; winter interest **Height:** 3–5' **Spread:** 24–36"
Hardiness: zones 4–9

Switch Grass
Panicum

A native to the prairie grasslands, switch grass naturalizes equally well in an informal border or in a natural meadow.

Growing

Switch grass thrives in **full sun, light shade** or **partial shade,** in **well-drained** soil of **average fertility**. It adapts to either moist or dry soils and tolerates conditions ranging from heavy clay to light, sandy soil. Cut switch grass back to 2–4" from the ground in early spring. The flower stems may break under heavy, wet snow or in exposed, windy sites.

Tips

Plant switch grass singly in small gardens, in large groups in spacious borders or at the edges of ponds or pools for a dramatic effect. The seedheads attract birds, and the foliage changes color in fall.

Recommended

P. virgatum (switch grass) is suited to wild meadow gardens. **'Heavy Metal'** is an upright plant with narrow, steely blue foliage flushed with gold and burgundy in fall. **'Prairie Sky'** is an arching plant with deep blue foliage. **'Shenandoah'** (red switch grass) has red-tinged, green foliage that turns burgundy in fall.

The delicate, airy panicles of switch grass fill gaps in the garden border, and they can be cut for fresh or dried arrangements.

Features: clumping habit; green, blue or burgundy foliage; airy panicles of flowers; fall color; winter interest **Height:** 3–5' **Spread:** 30–36" **Hardiness:** zones 3–8

P. virgatum cultivar (above)
P. virgatum 'Heavy Metal' (below)

Vinca
Vinca

V. minor (above & below)

Vinca is an excellent, reliable, evergreen groundcover. Allow this easy-to-grow plant to spread through your shady garden. It makes a great living mulch under shrubs and larger perennials.

Growing
Grow vinca in **partial to full shade**. It grows in **any type** of soil, but it turns yellow if the soil is too dry or the sun is too hot. Divide vinca in early spring or mid- to late fall or whenever it becomes overgrown. One plant can cover almost any size of area.

Tips
Vinca is an attractive groundcover in a shrub border, under trees or on a shady bank. It is shallow rooted and able to out-compete weeds but won't interfere with deeper-rooted shrubs. It also prevents soil erosion.

Vinca can be sheared back hard in early spring. The sheared-off ends may have rooted along the stems. These rooted cuttings may be potted and given away as gifts or may be introduced to new areas of the garden.

Recommended
V. minor forms a low, loose mat of trailing stems. Purple or blue flowers are borne in a flush in spring and sporadically throughout summer. **'Alba'** bears white flowers. **'Atropurpurea'** produces reddish purple flowers. **Bowles Series** plants have flowers in shades of white and blue.

Also called: lesser periwinkle, myrtle
Features: trailing foliage; mid-spring to fall flowers in purple, blue, white or reddish purple
Height: 4–8" **Spread:** indefinite
Hardiness: zones 4–8

Glossary

Acidic soil: soil with a pH lower than 7.0

Annual: a plant that germinates, flowers, sets seed and dies in one growing season

Alkaline soil: soil with a pH higher than 7.0

Basal foliage: leaves that form from the crown, at the base of the plant

Bract: a modified leaf at the base of a flower or flower cluster

Corm: a bulb-like, food-storing, underground stem, resembling a bulb without scales

Crown: the part of the plant at or just below soil level where the shoots join the roots

Cultivar: a cultivated plant variety with one or more distinct differences from the species, e.g., in flower color or disease resistance

Deadhead: to remove spent flowers to maintain a neat appearance and encourage a longer blooming season

Direct sow: to sow seeds directly in the garden

Dormancy: a period of plant inactivity, usually during winter or unfavorable conditions

Double flower: a flower with an unusually large number of petals

Espalier: a tree trained from a young age to grow on a single plane—often along a wall or fence

Genus: a category of biological classification between the species and family levels; the first word in a scientific name indicates the genus

Grafting: a type of propagation in which a stem or bud of one plant is joined onto the rootstock of another plant of a closely related species

Hardy: capable of surviving unfavorable conditions, such as cold weather or frost, without protection

Hip: the fruit of a rose, containing the seeds

Humus: decomposed or decomposing organic material in the soil

Hybrid: a plant resulting from natural or human-induced cross-breeding between varieties, species or genera

Neutral soil: soil with a pH of 7.0

Offset: a horizontal branch that forms at the base of a plant and produces new plants from buds at its tips

Panicle: a compound flower structure with groups of flowers on short stalks

Perennial: a plant that takes three or more years to complete its life cycle

pH: a measure of acidity or alkalinity; the soil pH influences availability of nutrients for plants

Rhizome: a root-like, food-storing stem that grows horizontally at or just below soil level, from which new shoots may emerge

Rootball: the root mass and surrounding soil of a plant

Seedhead: dried, inedible fruit that contains seeds; the fruiting stage of the inflorescence

Self-seeding: reproducing by means of seeds without human assistance, so that new plants constantly replace those that die

Semi-double flower: a flower with petals in two or three rings

Single flower: a flower with a single ring of typically four or five petals

Species: the fundamental unit of biological classification; the entity from which cultivars and varieties are derived

Standard: a shrub or small tree grown with an erect main stem, accomplished either through pruning and training or by grafting the plant onto a tall, straight stock

Sucker: a shoot that comes up from the root, often some distance from the plant; it can be separated to form a new plant once it develops its own roots

Tender: incapable of surviving the climatic conditions of a given region and requiring protection from frost or cold

Tuber: the thick section of a rhizome bearing nodes and buds

Variegation: foliage that has more than one color, often patched or striped or bearing leaf margins of a different color

Variety: a naturally occurring variant of a species

Index of Recommended Species Plant Names

Main entries are in **boldface**; botanical names are in *italics*.

Acer, 92
Actinidea, 123
Adiantum, 161
Aesculus, 85
Ajuga, 151
Allium (bulb), *132*
Allium (herb), *142*
Alum root. *See* Coral bells, 49
Amelanchier, 99
Amsonia, 43
Anemone, 57
Anethum, 143
Angel wings. *See* Angelonia, 11
Angelonia, 11
Arborvitae, 69
Aristolochia, 122
Artemisia, 149
Asclepias, 46
Aster, 40
  aromatic, 40
  New England, 40
  New York, 40
Astilbe, 41
  Arend's, 41
  Chinese, 41
  star, 41
Azalea. *See* Rhododendron, 97
Bacopa, 12
Bald cypress, 70
Baptisia, 51
Barberry, 71
  Japanese, 71
Barrenwort. *See* Bishop's
  hat, 152
  red, 152
Basil, 141
Basswood. *See* Linden, 90
Bat face. *See* Cuphea, 20
Beech, 72
  American, 72
  European, 72
Begonia, 13
  rex, 13
  wax, 13
Berberis, 71
Betula, 98
Bishop's hat, 152
Black gum, 73
Black lily turf. *See* Mondo

  grass, 164
Black tupelo. *See* Black gum,
  73
Black-eyed Susan (annual), **14**
Black-eyed Susan (perennial), **42**
Black-eyed Susan vine, 119
Blue fescue, 153
Blue oat grass, 154
Blue sheep's fescue. *See* Blue
  fescue, 153
Blue spirea. *See* Bluebeard,
  74
Bluebeard, 74
Bluebeech. *See* Hornbeam,
  84
Bluebird. *See* Bluebeard, 74
Bluestar, 43
Boltonia, 44
Bottlebrush. *See* Fothergilla,
  80
Bower actinidia. *See* Hardy
  kiwi, 123
Boxwood, 75
Brunnera, 45
Buckeye. *See* Horsechestnut, 85
  bottlebrush, 85
  red, 85
Bugleweed. *See* Ajuga, 151
Butter daisy, 15
Butterfly weed, 46
Buxus, 75

Calamagrostis, 168
Calendula, 16
Calibrachoa, 28
Calycanthus, 76
Canna, 129
Canna lily, 129
Cardinal flower, 47
  blue, 47
Carefree Beauty, 109
Carefree Delight, 110
Carolina allspice, 76
Carpinus, 84
Caryopteris, 74
Catharanthus, 26
Catmint, 48
Cécile Brünner, 111

Cercidiphyllum, 88
Cercis, 96
Chamaecyparis, 79
Chasmanthium, 160
Chionanthus, 81
Chives, 142
Christmas fern, 155
Cigar flower. *See* Cuphea, 20
Cinnamon fern. *See* Flowering fern, 158
Clematis, 120
  Jackman, 120
Cleome, 17
Clethra, 104
Climbing hydrangea, 121
Coleus, 18
Compass plant. *See* Rosinweed, 64
Coneflower. *See* Black-eyed
  Susan, 14
Coneflower. *See* Purple coneflower, 63
Coral bells, 49
Cornus, 78
Cosmos, 19
  annual, 19
  yellow, 19
Cotinus, 100
Crabapple, 77
Crocus, 130
Cup plant. *See* Rosinweed, 64
Cuphea, 20
Cutleaf coneflower. *See*
  Black-eyed Susan, 42

Daffodils, 131
Dahlberg daisy, 21
Daylily, 50
Dead nettle, 156
  spotted, 156
Dill, 143
Dogwood, 78
  American, 78
  Chinese, 78
  flowering, 78
  red-osier, 78
  red-twig, 78
Dortmund, 112
Dusty miller, 157

Dutchman's pipe, 122
smooth, 122
woolly, 122

Eastern arborvitae. *See*
Arborvitae, 69
Eastern white cedar. *See*
Arborvitae, 69
Echinacea, 63
Echinacea. *See* Purple cone-
flower, 63
Egyptian bean. *See* Hyacinth
bean, 125
English marigold. *See* Calen-
dula, 16
Epimedium, 152
Eranthis, 140
Eulalia. *See* Miscanthus, 163
European cranberrybush. *See*
Viburnum, 106
Everblooming Dr. W. Van
Fleet. *See* New Dawn, 116

Fagus, 72
Fairy. *See* The Fairy, 117
False cypress, 79
golden threadleaf, 79
False indigo, 51
False spirea. *See* Astilbe, 41
False sunflower, 52
Fan flower, 22
Fée des Neiges. *See* Iceberg,
114
Feerie. *See* The Fairy, 117
Festuca, 153
Fiddlehead fern. *See* Ostrich
fern, 166
Firecracker plant. *See*
Cuphea, 20
Flower Carpet, 113
Flowering fern, 158
Flowering onion, 132
Flowering tobacco. *See* Nico-
tiana, 29
Fothergilla, 80
dwarf, 80
large, 80
Fountain grass, 159
annual, 159
dwarf perennial, 159
red annual, 159
Fringe tree, 81
white, 81

Galanthus, 136
Garden verbena. *See* Verbena,
37
Geranium, 23
ivy-leaved, 23
scented, 23
zonal, 23
Giant onion. *See* Flowering
onion, 132
Globe amaranth, 24
Gloriosa daisy. *See* Black-
eyed Susan, 14
Golden fleece. *See* Dahlberg
daisy, 21
Golden garlic. *See* Flowering
onion, 132
Golden rain tree, 82
Goldenrod, 53
Gomphrena, 24
Guelder-rose. *See* Viburnum,
106

Hairy awn muhly. *See* Muh-
lygrass, 165
Hamamelis, 108
Hardy kiwi, 123
Helictotrichon, 154
Heliopsis, 52
Hellebore, 54
bear's foot, 54
stinking, 54
Helleborus, 54
Hemerocallis, 50
Heuchera, 49
Holly, 83
American, 83
Honeysuckle, 124
coral, 124
goldflame, 124
trumpet, 124
Hornbeam, 84
American, 84
European, 84
Horsechestnut, 85
red, 85
Hosta, 55
Hyacinth bean, 125
Hyacinth, 133
Hyacinthoides, 137
Hyacinthus, 133
Hydrangea (shrub), 86
Hydrangea (vine), 121
Hydrangea, 86
bigleaf, 86

oakleaf, 86
panicle, 86
smooth, 86

Iceberg, 114
Ilex, 83
Impatiens, 25
busy Lizzie, 25
New Guinea, 25
Indian bean. *See* Hyacinth
bean, 125
Inkberry. *See* Holly, 83
Inland sea oats, 160
Ipomoea, 36
Iris, 56
Ironwood. *See* Hornbeam, 84
Itea, 105

Japanese anemone, 57
**Japanese hydrangea vine,
126**
Japanese silver grass. *See* Mis-
canthus, 163
Johnny-jump-up. *See* Viola,
38
Juneberry. *See* Serviceberry,
99
Juniper, 87
Chinese, 87
creeping, 87
Japanese garden, 87
singleseed, 87
Juniperus, 87

Katsura tree, 88
Knockout, 115
Koelreuteria, 82
Kolomikta actinidia. *See*
Hardy kiwi, 123

Lablab bean. *See* Hyacinth
bean, 125
Lablab, 125
Lablab. *See* Hyacinth bean,
125
Lamb's ears, 58
Lamium, 156
Lathyrus, 128
Lavandula, 144
Lavender, 144
English, 144
Lenten rose. *See* Hellebore, 54
Lesser periwinkle. *See* Vinca,
170

Leucojum, 138
Lilac, 89
 Korean, 89
Lilium, 134
Lily leek. *See* Flowering
 onion, 132
Lily, 134
 oriental, 134
Linden, 90
 American, 90
 littleleaf, 90
 silver, 90
Lindera, 101
Lobelia, 47
Lobularia, 35
Lonicera, 124

Madagascar periwinkle, 26
Magnolia, 91
 southern, 91
 sweetbay, 91
Maiden grass. *See* Miscan-
 thus, 163
Maidenhair fern, 161
Maltese rose. *See* Cécile
 Brünner, 111
Malus, 77
Maple, 92
 full moon, 92
 Japanese, 92
 purpleblow, 92
 threeflower, 92
Marigold, 27
 African, 27
 American, 27
 Aztec, 27
 French, 27
 triploid, 27
Marjoram. *See* Oregano, 145
Matteuccia, 166
Maypop. *See* Passion flower, 127
Mazus, 162
 creeping, 162
Meadow rue, 59
 columbine, 59
 lavender mist, 59
Medallion flower. *See* Butter
 daisy, 15
Melampodium, 15
Mexican heather. *See*
 Cuphea, 20
Michaelmas daisy. *See* Aster, 40
Milkweed. *See* Butterfly
 weed, 46

Million bells, 28
Miscanthus, 163
Missouri coneflower. *See*
 Black-eyed Susan, 42
Mist grass. *See* Muhlygrass,
 165
Mondo Grass, 164
 black, 164
Moss rose. *See* Portulaca, 33
Muhlenbergia, 165
Muhlygrass, 165
 pink, 165
 purple, 165
Musclewood. *See* Hornbeam,
 84
Myrtle. *See* Vinca, 170

Narcissus, 131
Nepeta, 48
New Dawn, 116
Nicotiana, 29
Nierembergia, 30
Ninebark, 93
 common, 93
Nodding onion. *See* Flower-
 ing onion, 132
Northern maidenhair fern.
 See Maidenhair fern, 161
Nyssa, 73

Oak, 94
 scarlet, 94
 white, 94
 willow, 94
Ocimum, 141
Ophiopogon, 164
Orange sunflower. *See* False
 sunflower, 52
Oregano, 145
 Greek, 145
Origanum, 145
Osmunda, 158
Ostrich fern, 166
Ox eye. *See* False sunflower,
 52

Paeonia, 60
Panicum, 169
Pansy. *See* Viola, 38
Parsley, 146
 Italian, 146
Passiflora, 127
Passion flower, 127
Pelargonium, 23

Pennisetum, 159
Peony, 60
Perennial salvia, 61
Perovskia, 65
Persian shield, 31
Petroselinum, 146
Petunia, 32
 grandiflora, 32
 milliflora, 32
 multiflora, 32
Physocarpus, 93
Picea, 102
Pincushion flower, 62
Pine, 95
 lacebark, 95
Pineapple shrub. *See* Caro-
 lina allspice, 76
Pink hair grass. *See* Muhly-
 grass, 165
Pinus, 95
Plantain lily. *See* Hosta, 55
Pleurisy root. *See* Butterfly
 weed, 46
Polystichum, 155
Porcupine grass. *See* Miscan-
 thus, 163
Portulaca, 33
Pot marigold. *See* Calendula,
 16
Prairie dropseed, 167
Purple coneflower, 63
Purple ornamental millet.
 See Fountain grass, 159

Quercus, 94

Redbud, 96
 eastern, 96
Reed grass, 168
 feather, 168
 Foerster's feather, 168
Rhododendron, 97
Rhus, 103
River birch, 98
 black, 98
 red, 98
Rocky Mountain bee plant.
 See Cleome, 17
Rosa, 109–118
Rosemary, 147
Rosinweed, 64
Rosmarinus, 147
Royal fern. *See* Flowering
 fern, 158

Rudbeckia (annual), *14*
Rudbeckia (perennial), *42*
Rushgrass. *See* Prairie dropseed, 167
Russian Sage, 65

Sage (annual). *See* Salvia, 34
  blue, 34
  mealy cup, 34
  scarlet, 34
  Texas, 34
Sage (herb), **148**
Sage (perennial). *See* Perennial sage, 61
  azure, 61
  violet, 61
Salvia (annual), *34*
Salvia (herb), *148*
Salvia (perennial), *61*
Salvia, 34
Saskatoon. *See* Serviceberry, 99
Scabiosa, 62
Scaevola, 22
Schizophragma, 126
Scilla, 135
Sedum, 66
  autumn joy, 66
Senecio, 157
Serviceberry, 99
  apple, 99
  common, 99
  downy, 99
Shadberry. *See* Serviceberry, 99
Siberian bugloss. *See* Brunnera, 45
Siberian squill, 135
Silphium, 64
Smokebush, 100
  purple, 100
Snowdrop, 136
  common, 136
  giant, 136
Solenostemon, 18
Solidago, 53
Sour gum. *See* Black gum, 73
Spanish bluebells, 137
Spanish squill. *See* Spanish bluebells, 137
Spicebush, 101
Spicebush. *See* Carolina allspice, 76
Spider flower. *See* Cleome, 17
Spike speedwell, 67

Sporobolus, 167
Spruce, 102
  Colorado, 102
  Norway, 102
  white, 102
Stachys, 58
Stonecrop. *See* Sedum, 66
  gold moss, 66
  showy, 66
  tow-row, 66
Strawberry bush. *See* Carolina allspice, 76
Strobilanthes, 31
Sumac, 103
  flameleaf, 103
  fragrant, 103
  shining, 103
  staghorn, 103
Summer snapdragon. *See* Angelonia, 11
Summer snowflake, 138
Summersweet clethra, 104
Sutera, 12
Swamp milkweed. *See* Butterfly weed, 46
Sweet alyssum, 35
Sweet pea, 128
  perennial, 128
Sweet pepperbush. *See* Summersweet clethra, 104
Sweet potato vine, 36
Sweet shrub. *See* Carolina allspice, 76
Sweetheart rose. *See* Cécile Brünner, 111
Sweetspire, 105
Sweetspire. *See* Summersweet clethra, 104
Switch grass, 169
  red, 169
Syringa, 89

Tagetes, 27
Tarragon, 149
  French, 149
  German, 149
Taxodium, 70
Thalictrum, 59
The Fairy, 117
The New Dawn. *See* New Dawn, 116
The Thornless Rose. *See* Zéphrine Drouhin, 118
Thuja, 69

Thunbergia, 119
Thyme, 150
  common, 150
  lemon-scented, 150
Thymophylla, 21
Thymus, 150
Tilia, 90
Tiny mice. *See* Cuphea, 20
Toad lily, 68
  Japanese, 68
Trailing petunia. *See* Million bells, 28
Tricyrtis, 68
Tulipa, 139
Tulip, 139

Variegated kiwi vine. *See* Hardy kiwi, 123
Variegated maiden grass. *See* Miscanthus, 163
Verbena, 37
Veronica, 67
Viburnum, 106
  doublefile, 106
  Korean spice, 106
Vinca rosea. *See* Madagascar periwinkle, 26
Vinca, 170
Viola, 38
Virgin's bower. *See* Clematis, 120

Weigela, 107
Wild onion. *See* Flowering onion, 132
Willow bluestar. *See* Bluestar, 43
Windflower. *See* Japanese anemone, 57
Winter aconite, 140
Winterberry. *See* Holly, 83
Witchhazel, 108
  Ozark, 108
  vernal, 108
Wood hyacinth. *See* Spanish bluebells, 137
Woolly betony. *See* Lamb's ears, 58
Yellow archangel. *See* Dead nettle, 156
Zebra grass. *See* Miscanthus, 163
Zéphrine Drouhin, 118
Zinnia, 39
  Mexican, 39

Author Biographies

Anita Joggerst grew up with plants and animals on the family farm. As the Beginning Gardener columnist in the *St. Louis Post-Dispatch*, she enjoys sharing her knowledge and experience with novice gardeners, encouraging them to try native plants. She is a Missouri Certified Nursery Professional and a Master Gardener.

Veteran garden writer **Don Williamson** is the co-author of several popular gardening guides. He has a degree in horticultural technology and extensive experience in the design and construction of annual and perennial beds in formal landscape settings.

Author Acknowledgments

Thanks to Lone Pine Publishing and Don Williamson for this enjoyable opportunity. Also thanks to the Missouri gardeners who ask the questions that lead me to the research, always pushing me to learn something new. Special thanks to Chip Tynan of the Missouri Botanical Garden, who imparts his vast horticultural knowledge with great wit and wisdom, and to my sister, Joyce Roth, and my cousin, Rita Nieman, my greatest supporters.

—*Anita Joggerst*

I am blessed to work with many wonderful people, including my very knowledgeable and resourceful friend Anita Joggerst, and the great folks at Lone Pine Publishing. I also thank the Creator.

—*Don Williamson*